C for Pascal Programmers

C for Pascal Programmers

T. D. Brown, Jr.

Silicon Press
25 Beverly Road
Summit, NJ 07901, USA

Silicon Press
25 Beverly Road
Summit, NJ 07901, USA

Printing 9 8 7 6 5 4 3 2 1   Year 91 90 89 88
First Edition (Typeset on a HP LaserJet + using TPLUS/LJ)

Ada is a trademark of the U. S. Government, AJPO.
Apple is a trademark of Apple Computers.
IBM is a registered trademark of IBM.
Lattice is a registered trademark of Lattice, Inc.
MS is a trademark of the Microsoft Corporation.
Turbo Pascal is a registered trademark of Borland International.
UNIX is a registered trademark of AT&T.
VAX is a registered trademark of DEC.

Library of Congress Cataloging-in-Publication Data

Brown, T. D.
  C for Pascal Programmers / T. D. Brown, Jr.
     p.   cm.
Bibliography: p.
Includes index.
ISBN 0-9615336-4-1
1. C (Computer program language)   I. Title
QA76.73.C15B78 1988
005.13´3--dc19   87-26516
                                          CIP

BOOK EXAMPLES ON DISKETTE
For a diskette (in MS-DOS format) containing the source for the programs given in this book, send US $20.00 (includes shipping and handling) to

Silicon Press
25 Beverly Road
Summit, NJ 07901, USA

CONTENTS

PREFACE

This book is written especially for fluent Pascal programmers interested in learning C. It is not a beginning C book, for it assumes that the reader is familiar with basic programming concepts and wants to learn, not just the C syntax, but how to program well in C. The goal is not to teach the reader how to write Pascal programs in C but, instead, to teach C programming paradigms. The book focuses on effective C programming using programming techniques that make the best use of C facilities.

Now a bit about the background of Pascal and C. We will first discuss Pascal and then C. Pascal is a widely used programming language that is easy to learn and use. It was designed in 1971 by Professor N. Wirth of the Technical University of Zurich. Although Pascal was designed primarily as a language for teaching programming, it is now used for a wide range of applications—from systems programming to writing business software. Pascal has had a significant impact on modern programming language design and concepts. In this context, no recent language even comes close to Pascal. The only language that could be said to have had a greater impact than Pascal is FORTRAN, but that was in the 1950s.

If Pascal is such an important programming language that is used for a large variety of applications, then why not continue to program in Pascal? As a response to this question, here is a quote from B. Kernighan, a well-known computer scientist [Feue84]:

> *Pascal may be an admirable language for teaching beginners how to program ... But in its standard form ... Pascal is not adequate for writing real programs. It is suitable only for small, self-contained programs that have only trivial interactions with their environment and that make no use of any software written by anyone else.*

A word of caution. The operative phrase in the above criticism is "standard form". By this Kernighan is referring to the standard versions of Pascal, i.e., ISO Pascal* [Coop83] and Pascal as defined in the *Pascal User Manual and*

Report [Jens74], which we shall call J&W Pascal. Many Pascal compilers remedy the shortcomings of standard Pascal by extending the language to make it suitable for writing real programs, especially large ones. Unfortunately, each Pascal compiler implements its own set of extensions which can make program portability, an extremely important issue, non-trivial and expensive. Moreover, many Pascal compilers do not implement extensions that address all or most of the shortcomings of Pascal.

C is an excellent language for serious professional programming. Like Pascal, C is also an extremely popular language. According to *Byte* magazine (August 1983)

> *The C language provides a new standard for portability in a computer world characterized by a plethora of processors. ... Perhaps most aptly described as a "medium-level" programming language, C is a powerful tool in the hands of the professional programmer.*

C was designed by Dennis Ritchie, circa 1972, as a high-level replacement for assembly language programming. It was initially made popular by the UNIX^{TM} system which is now a dominating force in the multi-user operating system market (the UNIX system and its utilities are written in C). However, C's recent surge in popularity is entirely due to its own strengths and capabilities. C was used in the past primarily by professional programmers and in the universities. But now, it is the language of choice for serious programmers for just about every type of application and on all types of computers: from PCs to mainframes. In fact, most major microcomputer and software manufacturers use C for writing systems software [Byte83]. The primary reason for the current popularity of C is that it allows programmers to write portable programs while taking advantage of the characteristics of the underlying processor [Byte83].

The de facto C standard is the language defined in the *C Reference Manual* that is contained in *The C Programming Language* [Kern78]. We shall refer to this definition of C as K&R C. Most C compilers usually implement at least K&R C. To ensure more compatibility between compilers, C is now being modified in preparation to its being adopted as an ANSI standard. We shall use the term ANSI C to refer to the ANSI version of C. ANSI C, unlike K&R C, will be a formally recognized C standard. Official documents describing the preliminary version of ANSI C are now available. For the

---

* ANSI Pascal [ANSI83] is a subset of ISO Pascal.

interested reader, the book entitled *A C Reference Manual* [Harb84] is a very good source of detailed C syntax and semantics, and C features implemented by most compilers.

C is normally used in conjunction with a standard library that contains essential and important utility functions such as those for performing input and output. Until recently, these functions were not considered to be part of C. Instead, these and other utility functions were considered to be part of the environment provided by the C compiler or the operating system. For example, K&R C assumes the presence of the standard C library functions that are normally supplied by the UNIX system C compiler; however, K&R C does not describe the standard library functions [Kern78]. On the other hand, ANSI C considers the standard library functions to be part of the "C environment" and, therefore, describes them along with the definition of C. Many of these functions are described in *A C Reference Manual* [Harb84] and in the documentation provided with C compilers. Each C compiler is expected to provide these functions as part of its standard C library.

1. C COMPILERS, SOFTWARE & OTHER RESOURCES

Numerous C compilers are now available for the IBM PC and compatibles, and for almost all other types of computer systems. Here is a partial list of some well known C compilers (in alphabetical order):

- Aztec
- Borland International ("Turbo C")
- Computer Innovations
- DeSmet
- Lattice
- Mark Williams
- Microsoft
- Whitesmiths

C compilers are quite inexpensive; their prices range from about forty US dollars to several hundred US dollars. MIX Software sells a reasonable C compiler for the IBM PC that implements the full K&R C for $39.95, which is an amazingly low price! For a comparison of some of the IBM-PC C compilers, see an article by Phraner in the August 1983 issue of *Byte* [Phra83].

Countless software tools and packages are available for the C programmer. To find tools that meet your needs, look at some of the advertisements in recent issues of magazines such as *Byte*, *UNIX Review* and the *C Journal*. For example, in a recent issue of *Byte*, C libraries for multitasking, scientific programming, screen graphics, and database utilities were being advertised by a single software company!

C is the theme of the August 1983 issue of *Byte* magazine. Although somewhat outdated now, it is still a valuable resource handbook for the C programmer. This issue contains articles about C, the use of C for software development, comparison of C compilers, survey of C resources and an annotated bibliography of the C language. Another valuable handbook is the book entitled *Comparing & Assessing Programming Languages* [Feue84]. This book is a collection of articles comparing C and Pascal with each other and with the Ada^{TM} language. It contains a wealth of information about the differences between these languages.

2. C AND PASCAL DISCUSSED IN THIS BOOK

K&R C is the C discussed in this book along with appropriate comments about the forthcoming ANSI C, and the Pascal facilities discussed in this book are those found in J&W Pascal and ISO Pascal [Coop83]. We shall use the term "standard C" to refer to both K&R C and ANSI C, and the term "standard Pascal" to refer to both J&W Pascal and ISO Pascal.

There are many differences between K&R C and the proposed ANSI C. For example, ANSI C will require the user to specify parameter types in function declarations for better type checking, and single precision values will not be automatically converted to double precision values when they are passed as arguments to functions. The main difference between J&W Pascal and ISO Pascal is that ISO Pascal supports the notion of conformant arrays which allows, in different subprogram calls, arrays of different sizes to be passed as arguments corresponding to the same subprogram parameter. ANSI Pascal [ANSI83; Coop83] is essentially the same as ISO Pascal, but it does not support conformant arrays. In addition to referring to standard Pascal and C, we shall also refer to the facilities provided by Turbo Pascal and Lattice C compilers which are used for compiling, running, and testing the examples shown in this book.

3. GOALS OF THIS BOOK

This book can be used as a text book by Pascal programmers who want to teach themselves C or in an advanced C programming course for students who already know Pascal. It is not a first book on C and is not meant for those new to the programming discipline because it assumes that the readers are well versed in the science of programming. Consequently, there is essentially no discussion of the semantics of basic programming concepts such as assignment, expression evaluation, loops, and so forth. The focus of this book is on C programming and not on the C language syntax.

4. ORGANIZATION OF THE BOOK

The first chapter familiarizes the reader with the C programming language by showing several Pascal programs along with the corresponding C programs. These C programs are explained in detail along with comments about the ways in which C differs from Pascal.

The first chapter is followed by chapters and an appendix dealing with the following topics:

- Types and variables.
- Operators and expressions.
- Statements and input/output.
- Functions and files.
- Pointers.
- C preprocessor.
- Large examples.
- Library functions.

Each chapter is interlaced with numerous examples due to the author's conviction that learning programming is facilitated by the reading and understanding of examples. This is no different from other fields. For example, we learn good writing techniques by reading the works of good authors. Whenever appropriate, relevant documents, which are listed in the bibliography, are cited in the text (the citations are enclosed within square brackets).

The examples given in this book are real examples or close approximations thereof; they are not just toy examples. They can be used directly or as components of more elaborate programs. All the examples given in this book have been tested and are available in diskette form from Silicon Press. To facilitate the use of this diskette, the names of the header and source files which contain the code of the examples are given in this book.

T. D. Brown, Jr.

CHAPTER 1

INTRODUCTION

C is a general-purpose programming language designed especially for writing efficient and portable programs. C was designed by Dennis Ritchie, circa 1972, at the world famous AT&T Bell Laboratories, which is also where the popular UNIX system was designed. The goal of C was to replace assembly language programming that used to dominate programming at AT&T Bell Laboratories. C has not only surpassed this goal but has also succeeded far beyond its anticipated use. C is now used just about everywhere. Its influence extends from academic institutions to software houses and to personal computer users.

C is a compact programming language that offers a large spectrum of advanced programming facilities for program and data structuring. It is a versatile and flexible programming language that can be used for a wide range of application domains—from writing device controllers to writing database systems. C is routinely used for systems programming and in applications where efficiency and portability is important. C programs are easy to port because of the relatively high degree of standardization. Most compilers implement a standard version of the C language called K&R C [Kern78].

This book focuses primarily on the facilities specified in K&R C, and those in J&W Pascal and in ISO Pascal.* Whenever appropriate, comments will be made about additional (non standard) facilities provided by the Turbo Pascal and the Lattice C compilers.

---

* Note that the ANSI Pascal standard is essentially the same as the ISO Pascal standard except that it does not have the "conformant arrays" facility. Conformant arrays allow arrays of different sizes to be passed, in different calls, to the same subprogram as arguments corresponding to the same parameter.

As of now there is no formal standard for C. An effort to produce an ANSI standard version of C has been in progress for several years and the "ANSI C" standard should be forthcoming in the near future.

1

One final comment before we start discussing C. Because Pascal and C were designed for extremely different reasons—Pascal for teaching and C for replacing assembly language programming—one would expect them to be quite different. But surprisingly, although there are differences, Pascal and C have much in common. For example, both have similar data types and control statements. The main difference between the two languages is their type philosophy. Pascal's philosophy is to be strict and rigorous in enforcing typing rules, whereas C takes the view that the programmer knows best and allows the programmer to bypass the typing mechanism in a convenient manner. Compared to Pascal, C facilities are rather flexible thereby allowing the programmer to write compact and efficient programs.

1. GENERAL COMMENTS ABOUT C

A C program consists of declarations and definitions, a function named *main*, plus zero or more other functions. C makes a distinction between declarations and definitions [Kern78]: *declarations* specify identifier types but they do not allocate storage while *definitions* specify identifier types and, at the same time, they also allocate storage. Using C terminology, Pascal declarations would be called definitions.

A large C program is typically kept in several files. Some files may just contain declarations, in which case, they are called *header* files. Names of header files are, by convention, given the suffix *.h*. Other files may contain C functions and possibly, definitions and declarations; these files are called *source* files and their names are given the suffix *.c*. (Many C compilers will refuse to compile a file that does not have the *.c* suffix.) Typically, a C source file will contain one or more related functions, and related item definitions and declarations. Some of these items may be used for communication between functions in the same file and/or between functions in other files. Header files normally contain declarations that will be used in multiple files. Header files are included in source files or in other header files by using the C preprocessor *#include* statement. (The C preprocessor processes a C program before it is compiled by the C compiler. The C preprocessor is discussed in Chapter 7.) To produce an executable file, source files are compiled with the C compiler to produce object files which are then linked together with each other and with libraries using the system linker.

2. BASIC ELEMENTS OF C

2.1 C CHARACTER SET

Different C compilers may recognize different character sets, but all of them will recognize at least the following characters [Harb84]:

1. Upper-case and lower-case letters. Unlike Pascal, C is case sensitive which means that C distinguishes between upper- and lower-case characters. For example, C compilers do not consider the names *max* and *MAX* to be identical.

2. Ten decimal digits.

3. Special characters: ! % # ^ & * ( ) - _ + = ~ [} \ | ; : ' " { } , . < > / ?.

4. Blank.

5. Formatting characters: newline, backspace, horizontal tab, vertical tab, formfeed, and carriage return characters. Blank and formatting characters are collectively called the *white space* characters.

2.2 COMMENTS

C comments are similar to Pascal comments except that they begin with the character pair "/*" and are terminated with the character pair "*/". Comments can be inserted wherever a blank is allowed. Here is an example of a multi-line comment:

```
/*----------------------------------

    Pascal to C Conversion Program

--------------------------------*/
```

If you forget to terminate a comment, then the C compiler will treat the rest of the program until the next "*/" character pair, if any, as comments.

Most C compilers do not allow nested comments; some, like the Lattice C compiler, provide a compile-time option that allows comments to be nested.

2.3 STATEMENT TERMINATION

Like Pascal, C is a free-format language, that is, multiple statements can be placed on a single line or a single statement can span several lines.

In Pascal, semicolons are used to separate statements while in C they are used to terminate statements. All C statements, except executable statements that end with a right curly brace (i.e., compound statements), must be terminated with a semicolon.

Some computer scientists consider the use of a semicolon as a statement separator to be more elegant than its use as a statement terminator. However, in the case of beginning programmers, it has been observed that using the semicolon as a terminator is less error prone than using it as a separator.

2.4 IDENTIFIERS (NAMES)

Identifiers (names) are used as symbolic references for items such as constants, memory locations, types, and functions. A C identifier is a sequence of letters, digits, or underscores that begins with a letter or an underscore. By convention, identifiers that begin with an underscore are used only in system programs and not in application programs.

K&R C, like ISO Pascal, considers only the first 8 characters of an identifier to be significant, but many C compilers consider all the characters to be significant.

2.5 VARIABLES

As in Pascal, C variables are identifiers that are associated with memory locations. There is not much difference between the use of variables in the two languages. However, unlike Pascal variables, C variables can have different scopes and lifetimes and some classes of C variables can be given initial values in their definitions.

2.6 KEYWORDS

Some C identifiers, as in Pascal, are reserved words that cannot be used as user-defined identifiers in programs. Here is a list of the C keywords [Harb84].

```
auto        else        long        typedef
break       enum        register    union
case        extern      return      unsigned
char        float       short       void
continue    for         sizeof      while
default     goto        static
do          if          struct
double      int         switch
```

As in the case of the (predefined) Pascal standard identifiers, the names of C library functions should not be redefined if they are going to be used in the program.

3. A QUICK TOUR OF THE C LANGUAGE

The rest of this chapter is intended to give you a quick tour of the C language. We will write programs for four problems. For each problem, we will show you a Pascal program and then an equivalent C program. Because this book is intended for experienced Pascal programmers, the Pascal programs will not be explained in detail. These programs are straightforward, and the reader should not have any trouble understanding them. However, each C program will be followed by a detailed discussion including a comparison with the corresponding Pascal program. This discussion will also include comments about the differences between C and Pascal. The C concepts presented in this section will, of course, be discussed in depth in later chapters.

The best way to get comfortable in a new programming language is to get "hands-on" programming experience. Consequently, you should compile and run the C programs given in this book on your computer. Hands-on programming will not only make you conversant and comfortable with C quickly, but it will also "acclimatize" you to the C programming environment with the minimum of delay.

A word about the notation used in the text. Both Pascal and C programs will be shown in typewriter-like font. Italic font will be used when referring to both Pascal and C identifiers and their constructs in the text.

3.1 COMPUTING ACCRUED INTEREST EXAMPLE

The first problem involves writing a program to compute the interest paid by a bank on money deposited by the customer. Although different banks may pay the same simple interest rate, the "actual" or compound interest paid by them may be different. This is because the accumulated interest is computed and paid by different banks after different time periods. The more frequently the interest is paid, the more total interest you get, because you start getting interest on the interest itself sooner. For example, other things being equal, you will get more total interest from a bank that pays interest daily rather than from a bank that pays interest quarterly or yearly. (Paying the interest on a daily basis is called *daily compounding*.) The total interest paid by a bank can be computed by the formula

$$i = p*((1+r/(100*np))^{np*yrs} - 1)$$

where

- i is the total interest paid,
- p is the principal amount,
- r is the interest rate in percent,
- np is the number of periods in a year when interest is paid, and
- yrs is the number of years the money is kept on deposit.

First, we will take a look at the Pascal program (stored in file *int.p*):

```
program interest(input, output);
    var p, r, i: real;
        np, yrs: integer;
    function pow(x: real; n: integer): real;
        var result, a: real;
            i: integer;
    begin
        result := 1; a := x; i := n;
        {preserve relation "result*a**i=x**n"
         but move i to 0 so that "result=x**n";
        (note that ** denotes exponentiation) }
            while i > 0 do
            begin
                while not odd(i) do
                begin
                    i := i div 2;
                    a := a * a
                end;
                i := i - 1;
                result := result * a
            end;
        pow := result
    end;
begin
    write('principal?');
    readln(p);
    write('interest rate?');
    readln(r);
    write('no. of periods per year?');
    readln(np);
    write('years?');
    readln(yrs);
    i := p*(pow(1+r/(100*np), np*yrs)-1);
    writeln('total interest =  ', i:8:2)
end.
```

Now, we will take a look at the corresponding C program (stored in file *int.c*):

```
#include <stdio.h>
#include <math.h>
main()
{
    float p, r, i;
    int np, yrs;

    printf("principal?");
    scanf("%f", &p);
    printf("interest rate?");
    scanf("%f", &r);
    printf("no. of periods per year?");
    scanf("%d", &np);
    printf("years?");
    scanf("%d", &yrs);
    i = p*(pow(1+r/(100.0*np), (double) np*yrs)-1);
    printf("total interest = %g\n", i);
}
```

Even for this simple interest calculation problem, the corresponding Pascal and C programs differ substantially thus illustrating many differences between the two languages.

The outstanding difference between the C and Pascal programs is that the Pascal program is much larger. This is because Pascal does not provide an exponentiation facility; consequently the exponentiation function *pow* had to be written explicitly. It was not necessary to write *pow* in C because the standard math library supplied by all the C compilers contains *pow*. Unlike FORTRAN, PL/I, and other languages, neither Pascal nor C has an exponentiation operator. The exponentiation operator was not included in C and in Pascal by their designers on the grounds that this operator, unlike the other operators such as subtraction and division, does not correspond to a simple operation of the underlying computer.

Before discussing other differences between the two programs, let us first examine the above C program in detail. The first two lines (beginning with the character #) are C preprocessor statements. As mentioned earlier, every C program is processed by the C preprocessor before it is compiled. Although the C preprocessor is logically not part of the C compiler, for all practical purposes it is considered to be an integral part of every C compiler. The C preprocessor is typically used for things such as file inclusion and constant definitions (the preprocessor is discussed in detail in Chapter 7). The two *#include* instructions in the above C program are used to include files named *stdio.h* and *math.h* which contain the declarations of the C standard input and output functions, and the declarations of the math functions. Functions, like variables, should be declared (or defined) before they are used. Input and output functions are not built into the C language but are, instead, part of the standard C library *stdio*. The file containing the math library declarations is included for the declaration of the exponentiation function *pow*.

As mentioned earlier, by convention the *.h* suffix is used for C files that contain declarations. Such files are called *header* files.

Continuing our discussion of the C program, note the definition of function *main* which begins on line 3. Each C program must contain the distinguished function *main* because execution of a C program begins by executing this function. (Some C compilers allow the user to specify an alternative distinguished function; ANSI C prohibits this.) The body of the *main* function begins with the left curly brace (line 4) and is terminated by the right curly brace (last line of the program).

The first two lines within the body of function *main* are variable definition statements which define identifiers p, r, and i to be variables of type *float* (single precision) and identifiers *np* and *yrs* to be of type *int* (integer). After the variable definitions, there are four pairs of *printf* (output) and *scanf* (input) statements. To be precise, these statements are actually calls to standard library functions. Each of these *printf* statements (actually function calls) has only one argument: the string to be printed. In general, the *printf* function can take a variable number (at least one) of arguments. The first argument specifies the text to be printed and contains place holders for the other arguments which are all to be printed. The place holders also specify the formats to be used when printing the other arguments. The first argument of the *printf* function is called the format string.

The *scanf* statement is the input counterpart of the *printf* statement. Each of the *scanf* statements used in the above program has two arguments. The first argument in each of these *scanf* statements specifies that the value to be read is either a floating point value (*%f*) or an integer value (*%d*), and the second argument gives the address (memory location) of the variable where the value read is to be stored. (Note that the ampersand operator "&" extracts the address of its operand.)

After the four *printf* and *scanf* statement pairs, the C program has an assignment statement. Note that this statement contains a cast (a type conversion): the integer expression *np∗yrs* is converted to a double precision value to meet the requirements of function *pow*. The assignment statement is followed by another *printf* statement that prints a message and the value of variable i. As mentioned before, the first argument contains the text to be printed and format items specifying the format in which the other arguments are to be printed. In this case, format item "*%g*" specifies that argument i is to be printed in "*g*" format. Depending upon the value to be printed, the "*g*" format instructs the *printf* function to select the most appropriate of the floating point or the scientific formats to print the corresponding argument.

After printing variable *i*, the *printf* statement prints a newline character which is denoted by the two-character sequence "*n*". The backslash character is called the *escape character*. Printing the newline character causes the cursor (or print position) to skip to the beginning of the next line.

Assignment is an operator in C and not a statement as in Pascal. The value of an assignment expression is the value assigned to the variable on the left of the assignment operator. If the value of an expression is not used, then it is simply discarded. Moreover, appending a semicolon to any expression transforms the expression into a statement. This allows an assignment expression to be written like a statement; for example:

```
i = p*(pow(1+r/(100*np), np*yrs)-1);
```

3.1.1 DIFFERENCES BETWEEN THE PASCAL & C PROGRAMS. We will now compare the Pascal and C versions of the interest calculation program to illustrate some of the differences between the two languages:

1. As mentioned before, the most striking difference between the Pascal and C programs is that the Pascal program is much larger. This is because in the Pascal program the exponentiation function *pow* had to be written explicitly while the C program simply calls function *pow* which is contained in the math library provided by all C compilers.

2. In Pascal, the keyword *program* is used to indicate the main routine; on the other hand, in C the special name *main* indicates the main routine.

3. Names of the input and output files, including the standard input and output files, and all permanent files to be manipulated in a Pascal program must be specified in the *program* statement. In the case of C, the standard input, output, and error files are automatically made available to the programmer. Names of other files can be passed from the command line to the *main* function, or they can be read as input or constructed in the program itself. Different file names (strings) can be passed to different invocations of a C program, but to do this in a Pascal program will require modification of the *program* statement.

4. The order of declarations is important in standard Pascal but not in C (or in Turbo Pascal). Pascal declarations must come in the following order: labels, constants, types, variables, and functions and procedures. This order facilitates the compilation process but it is a nuisance for the programmer and detracts from program readability. For example, in the Pascal program the definition of *pow* separates the definitions of the main program variables from the statements that reference them.

5. The style of variable definitions is different in the two languages. In Pascal the variable identifiers are listed first followed by the type, whereas in C the type is listed first followed by the variable identifiers.

6. In Pascal curly braces or the "*(*" and "*)*" character pairs are used to delimit comments. Although not shown in this simple example, C comments are delimited by the character pairs "/*" and "*/".

7. Keywords *begin* and *end* are used in Pascal to enclose a group of statements (to form a compound statement) while curly braces are used in C.

8. Semicolons are used to separate statements in Pascal while in C semicolons are used as statement terminators. The use of semicolons as statement separators has been found to be error prone especially when learning programming. Learning to use semicolons as statement terminators is straightforward; just terminate each statement by a semicolon. Note that in C, there is one exception to this rule. When an executable statement (but not a declaration or definition) ends in right curly brace (i.e., a compound statement), then it is not followed by a semicolon.

9. In Pascal, single quotes are used to enclose strings and character literals (to be precise, character literals are strings consisting of a single character). In C double quotes are used to enclose string literals and single quotes to enclose character literals.

10. Input/output facilities are part of Pascal while in C they are provided as part of the standard library. This allows the Pascal compiler to automatically determine the item formats whereas in the case of C, the item formats must be explicitly supplied by the programmer. Pascal provides very limited facilities for formatted input and output, while C provides elaborate facilities.

11. The Pascal input procedure *readln* is passed the names of the variables where the input values are to be stored. On the other hand, the C input function *scanf* is passed the item format and the *addresses* of the variables where the input values are to be stored. C functions must be passed addresses of variables (except for array variables) if their values are to be changed in the function. This is because C does not have the notion of passing arguments by reference; all arguments are passed by value. Pointers are used to simulate passing arguments by reference. In case of arrays, it is not necessary to pass the address of the array because the value passed by the C compiler for an array variable is the address of the array.

12. The *writeln* procedure (instead of the *write* procedure) is used to print a new line in Pascal while in C a new line is printed by printing the newline character "\n". In C the newline character is just like any other character. In Pascal the newline character cannot be read or written explicitly, but new lines can be sensed using the end-of-line

function; special procedures must be used to explicitly skip to a new input or output line.

13. All Pascal functions and procedures must be nested within another function, another procedure or in the main program. In this example, the exponentiation *pow* is nested within the main program *interest*. C, on the other hand, does not allow nested functions (there are no procedures in C). The definition of a new function can be started after completing the definition of the previous function (if any). All functions are at the "same level". This means that it is not possible to define a function that is local to another function. In practice, the lack of local functions is rarely, if ever, felt by C programmers. As we shall discuss later, C has other facilities for controlling the scope of functions.

3.1.2 COMPILING & RUNNING C PROGRAMS. Let us now discuss the execution of the above C program. As mentioned above, the C version of the interest calculation program is stored in the file named *int.c*. For the purpose of illustration, we shall use the Lattice™ C compiler commands to compile and link C programs.

File *int.c* is compiled with the Lattice C compiler command *lc*:

```
lc int
```

The Lattice C compiler operates in two phases. The first phase program is called *lc1* and the second phase program is called *lc2*. These two programs can be explicitly invoked individually as follows:

```
lc1 int
lc2 int
```

The Lattice C compiler produces an object code (machine language) translation of the above interest calculation program and stores it in the file *int.obj*. Before the C program can be executed, it must be linked together with the C libraries containing the input and output functions and the math function *pow* that are used in *int.c*. The Lattice command *linkms* can be used to do this:

```
linkms int
```

This command invokes the MS-DOS linker *link* with the appropriate arguments including one that instructs it to link the program with the math library (specified by the *m* in *linkms*). Linking *int.obj* with the libraries produces the executable file named *int.exe*.

The C program can now be invoked by simply typing

```
int
```

which causes file *int.exe* to be executed.

3.2 FILE COPY EXAMPLE

The second problem involves writing a program to read input from the keyboard, and then print it on the display. By appropriately redirecting the input and the output, this program can also be used to display the contents of a file, store the keyboard input in a file and copy files.

First, the Pascal program (stored in file *c.p*):

```
{$B-}
program copytext(input, output);
    var c: char;
begin
    while not eof do
    begin
        while not eoln do
        begin
            read(c); write(c)
        end;
        readln; writeln
    end
end.
```

This program reads its input from the terminal and prints its output on the screen. Notice that Turbo Pascal requires the user to specify the "compiler directive"

```
{$B-}
```

to prevent procedure *read* from skipping to a new line after reading the specified variables. The default interpretation of *read* (without the use of the above compiler directive) does not conform to that specified in standard Pascal.

In standard Pascal, the end-of-file and end-of-line state cannot be read, but they can be sensed by using the boolean functions *eof* and *eoln*. Input can be read starting from a new line by using the *readln* procedure; output can be printed on a new line by using the *writeln* procedure. Turbo Pascal allows the end-of-line character to be read. This is non-standard, but it allows the program to be written simply as

```
{$B-}
program copytext(input, output);
    var c: char;
begin
    while not eof do
    begin
        read(c); write(c)
    end
end.
```

Pascal standard input and output can be redirected. However, in case of Turbo Pascal the user must modify the Pascal program to include appropriate compiler directives. This requires program recompilation because the same compiled code cannot be used to read from (write to) both the terminal and a disk file.

Now, the C program (stored in file *c.c*):

```c
#include <stdio.h>
main()
{
    int c;

    while ((c = getchar()) != EOF)
        putchar(c);
}
```

The C program reads characters, one at a time, from the standard input, i.e., the keyboard, and writes them on the standard output, i.e., the display. C input functions combine the linefeed and carriage return characters into one character called the newline character. C output functions do the reverse; that is, they translate a newline character to the linefeed and carriage return characters.

The above C program contains one definition, that of variable *c*, which is defined as an integer, and one executable statement, the *while* loop. The expression in the *while* loop includes a call to the input function *getchar*, which reads a character from the standard input. This is stored in the integer variable *c*. The loop (and consequently the program) terminates when function *getchar* returns –1. *EOF* is a symbolic constant defined as –1 in the header file *stdio.h* using a preprocessor *#define* statement (more on constant definitions in Chapter 7).

Notice that *EOF* is in upper case while everything else is in lower case. Unlike Pascal, C is *case sensitive*, that is, it does not treat upper- and lower-case letters as synonyms of each other. Traditionally, C programs are written predominantly using lower-case letters. Upper-case letters are used for preprocessor definitions (as in the case of *EOF*) and sometimes for user-defined type names.

Character variables are essentially integer variables. Character values can be stored in integer variables and non-negative integers in character variables. Variables used for storing characters read by functions such as *getchar* are defined as integer variables because these functions return a –1 to indicate the end of file. (Note that –1 does not correspond to the ASCII representation of any character.)

The body of the *while* loop consists of a single statement: a call to the function *putchar* which prints its character argument on the standard output.

Note that functions *getchar* and *putchar* are usually, but not always, implemented as macros (defined using the C preprocessor) for efficiency: minimization of execution time. Macros are discussed in Chapter 7.

Suppose the above C program is stored in file *c.c*. Then this program can be compiled and linked using the following Lattice C compiler commands

```
lc c
links c
```

which produce file *c.exe*, the executable version of *c.c*. This time the MS-DOS linker *link* is invoked using the command *links*, instead of the command *linkms*, because it is not necessary to link this program with the math library.

The executable program *c.exe* can be invoked in several different ways to make it do different things. For example, invoking it simply as

```
c
```

causes it to read characters from the terminal and print them on the monitor.

If input is redirected from a file, then program *c.exe* can be used to display a file on the monitor:

```
c  <source-file
```

If output is redirected to a file, then *c.exe* can be used to store characters typed at the keyboard in a file:

```
c  >target-file
```

If both input and output are redirected, then program *c.exe* can be used to copy files:

```
c  <source-file  >target-file
```

3.2.1 DIFFERENCES BETWEEN THE PASCAL & C PROGRAMS. Comparing the Pascal and C versions of the file copy program, we notice the following differences:

1. As mentioned before, in standard Pascal the end-of-file and end-of-line states cannot be read, but they can be sensed by using the boolean functions *eof* and *eoln*. Input can be read from a new line by using the *readln* procedure; output can be printed on a new line by using the *writeln* procedure. On the other hand, C treats the newline character* just like any other character, and functions indicate the end of file by

---

*   As mentioned earlier, C combines the linefeed and carriage return characters into a
      single character, the newline character.

returning –1. The newline character (denoted as "\n") can be read and written. The different ways in which Pascal and C treat newlines makes the standard Pascal program somewhat more complex (and bigger) than the C program.

2. Unlike Pascal, C does not treat input lines specially. C expects input to be a character stream and its input functions read one or more characters, as needed. Input of a newline character indicates transition to a new line. Different input functions treat newline characters differently; to cite an example, a function such as *getchar*, which is used to read one character at a time, will pass the newline character directly to the program. However, a function such as *scanf*, which is used for formatted input, will discard leading newline characters (and other "white-space" characters such as blanks and tabs) when it reads a number. *scanf* does not care whether or not the input contains the exact number of items needed by it. If there are more items on a line than it needs, then *scanf* just reads the number of items needed by it. On the other hand, if there are not enough items on the current line, then it will go on to successive input lines until it gets the items needed by it or until it encounters an end of file.

3. Variable *c* is declared as a character variable in Pascal but as an integer variable in C. This is because in C the input function *getchar* returns –1 to indicate that an end of file was encountered. –1 does not correspond to a legal character. Consequently, to store –1 properly, *c* must be defined as an integer and not as a character variable. Similarly, because function *getchar* may return a –1, it is declared (in the header file *stdio.h*) as an integer function.

   Characters are stored and treated in C as small integers that occupy one byte of storage. Thus, the character type *char* is often used in C programs for defining small integers.

4. Because assignment is an operator in C, it can be used within the *while* expression. Assignment in Pascal is a statement and cannot, therefore, be used within an expression.

3.3 POCKET CALCULATOR EXAMPLE

The third problem involves writing a calculator program to perform addition (+), subtraction (–), multiplication (*), and division (/). The calculator displays the "running" total in its internal accumulator after each of the above operations. Entering the character "c" clears the internal accumulator. The calculator is "turned off" by typing the control-break character which terminates the program.

Here is the Pascal version of the calculator program (stored in file *calc.p*):

```pascal
{calculator program}
{$B-}
program calculator(input, output);
    var result, opd: real;
        opr: char;
        error: boolean;
begin
    error := false;
    writeln('0');
    read(result); {first operand}
    while not error do
    begin
        read(opr); while opr = ' ' do read(opr);
        if opr = 'c'
        then
            begin
                writeln('0');
                read(result)
            end
        else if opr in ['+', '-', '*', '/']
            then
                begin
                    readln(opd);
                    case opr of
                        '+': result := result + opd;
                        '-': result := result - opd;
                        '*': result := result * opd;
                        '/': result := result / opd
                    end;
                    writeln(result)
                end
            else
                error := true
    end;
    writeln('***error***')
end.
```

Now here is the C version of the calculator program (stored in file *calc.c*):

```
/*calculator program*/

#include <stdio.h>
main()
{
    float result, opd;
    int opr;

    printf("   0\n");
    scanf("%f", &result);   /*first operand*/
    for (;;) {
        while (isspace(opr = getchar()))
            ;
        if (opr == 'c') {
            printf(" %g\n", result = 0);
            scanf("%f", &result);
        }
        else if (opr == '+' || opr == '-' ||
                 opr == '*' || opr == '/') {
            scanf("%f", &opd);
            switch (opr) {
                case '+':
                    result += opd; break;
                case '-':
                    result -= opd; break;
                case '*':
                    result *= opd; break;
                case '/':
                    result /= opd;
            }
            printf(" %g\n", result);
        }
        else {
            printf("***error***\n");
            exit(1);
        }
    }
}
```

The calculator program starts off by printing the string " $0\n$", that is, it prints a zero and then moves to a new line. The program then enters an infinite loop which is specified by a *for* statement of the form

```
for (;;)
{
  ...
}
```

The C *while* loop, like the one used inside the *for* loop, can also be used to specify an infinite loop that looks much like the infinite loop used in the Pascal version of the calculator program. Because C does not have a boolean type, the *while* expression will be some non-zero value, e.g., 1. Note that C interprets non-zero values as true and zero values as false.

The *while* loop nested inside the *for* loop reads characters until it encounters a "non-space" character. Here is how its execution proceeds. The *while* expression is evaluated first. Evaluation means calling function *getchar* to read a character from the standard input (the keyboard is the default standard input) and assigning it to the variable *opr*. The result of this assignment is the final value of *opr* which is then passed to function *isspace* (whose declaration is contained in the header file *ctype.h*). This function returns true (1) if its argument is one of the following characters: a blank, a tab, a carriage return, a newline, or a formfeed. Otherwise it returns false (0). If the *while* expression is true, then the null statement (denoted by the semicolon), which is the body of this loop, is executed; otherwise, the loop terminates.

Loops with null bodies are a peculiar C phenomenon. You will often encounter such loops in C programs. The loop expression does all the work while the loop body does nothing.

Following the *while* loop is the nested *if* statement which is of the form

```
if (opr == 'c')
    ...
else if (opr == '+' || opr == '-' ||
         opr == '*' || opr == '/')
    ...
else
    ...
```

Operator "==" is the C comparison operator. Be careful when using it because a common mistake is to leave out one of the "=" characters. A single "=" character denotes the assignment operator, and assignment, unlike in most other languages, is allowed in C expressions. The result of an assignment expression is the value assigned to the lefthand variable. Consequently, assigning a non-zero value means that the assignment expression will evaluate to true and assigning a zero value means that the assignment expression will evaluate to false.

Nested *if* statements can be used for multi-way branching. Like the *case* statement of Pascal, C also has another control structure called the *switch* statement for multi-way branching. The *switch* statement evaluates its expression and jumps to the alternative with a *case* label whose value matches that of the *switch* expression. Statements following the *case* label are then executed. Unlike the Pascal *case* statement, the execution of a *switch* statement alternative must be terminated explicitly by using a statement that changes the flow of control, e.g., by using a *break*, a *continue* or a *return* statement.

Let us now consider the *switch* statement in this program. The *switch* expression consists of just the variable *opr*. Depending upon the value of this variable, the value of *opr* is added to, subtracted from, multiplied with or divided into that of variable *result*, and the result of this operation is then stored in *result*.

The first statement after each *case* label is an assignment statement. In addition to the operator corresponding to the conventional form of assignment, C provides several other types of assignment operators. For example, the operator "+ =" adds its right operand to its left operand; the assignment statement

```
result += opd;
```

is equivalent to the assignment statement

```
result = result + opd;
```

After each of the first three assignment statements inside the *switch* statement is the *break* statement, which is used to exit from the *switch* statement. In the absence of the *break* statement, control will flow from one *switch* alternative to the next. Some programmers often exploit this "feature" for "efficiency" reasons, e.g., to avoid duplicating code. However, allowing control to flow from one alternative to another is dangerous because it can lead to errors. For example, statements can be changed in a *switch* alternative without realizing that control also flows to the changed alternative from the previous alternative.

In case the user of this calculator program types an invalid operator, the program is terminated by calling function *exit*. By convention, function *exit* is called with the value zero to indicate successful program completion; abnormal or failed program termination is indicated by calling *exit* with the value one. Function *exit* can also be called with other values to indicate other program completion states. The *exit* function should be used to terminate a program if program termination information is to be passed back to the program creator, i.e., the parent program (see your compiler reference manual for more details).

3.3.1 DIFFERENCES BETWEEN THE PASCAL & C PROGRAMS. Comparing the Pascal and C versions of the calculator program, we notice the following differences:

1. The Pascal program uses the boolean variable *error* to terminate the loop (and the program) if an illegal operator is used. In the C program, the *exit* function is used to terminate the program. Pascal and C programs can terminate by completing execution of the main program and the *main* function, respectively. However, a C program can also terminate by executing, anywhere in the program, the *exit*

statement and also by executing the *return* statement in the *main* function.

2. By using the boolean variable *error* in the Pascal program, the use of a *goto* statement to terminate the program is avoided. Although the C program appears not to have any *goto* statements, this observation is not quite true because the C program uses the *break* statement which is a restricted form of the *goto* statement (more later about the *break* statement).

    C provides several statements, such as the *break, continue* and *return* statements, for controlled jumps. Consequently, unlike as in the case of Pascal, the need for an explicit *goto* statement rarely arises. Note that, as illustrated in this example, most Pascal programmers avoid using *goto* statements by using extra variables.

3. There is no equivalent of the Pascal set type in C. This means that in C explicit comparisons must be done to test whether or not a variable is equal to any one value belonging to a set of values. For example, determining whether or not *opr* contains a legal operator value is done by comparing it explicitly with all possible legal operator values.

4. The Pascal *case* statement is safer than the C *switch* statement since there is no need to do an explicit jump at the end of each alternative. Although not illustrated in this example, the C *switch* statement is more flexible and convenient to use than the Pascal *case* statement because it provides a *default* alternative. This "catch all" alternative handles cases for which there is no label. Finally, in Pascal an error occurs if there is no alternative corresponding to the value of the *case* expression; on the other hand, if there is no alternative (including the *default* alternative) that matches the value of the *switch* expression, then the *switch* statement behaves like a null statement.

5. Unlike the Pascal *writeln* (or *write*) statement, the C *printf* statement with the "%g" format can automatically print a real value in either of the fixed point or scientific notations, depending upon which one is more appropriate.

3.4 DOUBLE-WORD CHECKER EXAMPLE

A common mistake that people make when entering text into a computer file with a text editor is to enter the same word twice in a row. Double words can be on the same line as in

```
Alice in in Wonderland
```

or on different lines as in

```
Alice in
in Wonderland
```

The problem is to write a program that finds occurrences of such double words in a file and then prints the numbers of the lines containing (at least one of) the double words.

For our purposes, we will define a word to be any continuous sequence of non-space characters on the same line. Although this definition simplifies writing of the double-word checker, it also means that we will not be able to detect double word occurrences such as the one illustrated in the following sentence:

```
She brought great news news.
```

This is because, according to our definition of a word, the second "news" will not be a word by itself; instead, it will be part of the word "news." because there is no blank space preceding the period. Refinements of the double-word checker program to cover the above situation and other situations not handled by it are left as an exercise for the reader.

Here is the Pascal version of the double-word checker (stored in file *double.p*):

```
{$B-,G512,P512,D-}
program double_word(input, output);
    const wl = 80;
    type wordtype = array[0..wl] of char;
    var next, last, blanks: wordtype;
        line_no, i: integer;
    function word(var s: wordtype): boolean;
                {if word found then return true;
                        otherwise return false}
        var c: char;
            i: integer;
            gotword: boolean;
    begin
        for i := 0 to wl do blanks[i] := ' ';
        i := 0; gotword := false;
        while not (eof or gotword) do
        begin
            while not (eoln or gotword) do
            begin
                read(c);
                if (c = ' ') and (i <> 0)
                then gotword := true
                else if c <> ' '
                        then begin
                            s[i] := c; i := i+1
                        end;
            end;
```

```
            if i <> 0 then gotword := true;
            if eoln
            then begin
                        readln;
                        line_no := line_no + 1
                  end
      end;
      word := gotword
   end;
begin
   line_no := 1;
   next := blanks; last := blanks;
   while word(next) do
   begin
      if next = last then
      begin
          write('double word **');
          i := 0;
          while last[i] <> ' ' do
          begin
              write(last[i]);
              i := i + 1
          end;
          writeln('** on line ', line_no)
      end;
      last := next;
      next := blanks
   end
end.
```

The first line contains compiler directives required by the Turbo Pascal compiler.

As we shall see, the most important difference between the Pascal and C versions of the double-word checker program is that the C program, unlike the Pascal program, is stored in three separate files. C programs can be partitioned into several files which can be independently compiled. The compiled components can then be linked (joined) together to produce the final executable program. Standard Pascal does not support independent compilation although many Pascal compilers (but not the Turbo Pascal compiler) support independent compilation on an ad hoc basis. Independent compilation is extremely important for developing large programs. With independent compilation, only those parts of a program that have been modified need to be recompiled; it is not necessary to recompile the whole program.

The three files containing the C program are *double.h*, *double.c*, and *word.c*. Header file *double.h* contains the declarations used in the other two files. Source files *double.c* and *word.c* contain the code for the main program which does the double word comparison, and for the function *word* which returns words from the input file (it disassembles the input file into a stream of words).

Each file containing C program text is equivalent to a *module*. (We shall use the terms file and module interchangeably.) Breaking up a program into small modules is important for writing large programs. First, information local to a module can be hidden from other modules. Second, it is easier to update and maintain small modules rather than large ones. Third, compiling (or editing) a small module is faster than compiling (or editing) a large module. Finally, after a program has been modified, only the modified modules and other modules that depend upon them need to be recompiled (this process can be automated by using a program called *make* which is available for IBM PC computers from the Microsoft Corporation).

Here are the contents of the declarations file *double.h*:

```
#include <stdio.h>
#define WL 80

extern int line_no;
```

The second line of the above file is the C preprocessor *#define* statement which defines *WL* to be a symbolic constant with the value 80. The program assumes that the maximum length of the words in the file is not going to be more than 80 characters, which is quite a reasonable assumption. In fact, the C program can be made more flexible by allowing it to accept words of arbitrary length.

The third line in the above header file is a blank line. As in Pascal programs, blank lines are often inserted in C programs to increase program readability. The C compiler ignores blank lines just as it ignores comments.

The fourth line is a C declaration which declares an external integer (*extern int*) variable, named *line_no*, that will be used for inter-function communication. These functions can be in the same file or in different files. If this global (external) variable is to be used only for intra-file inter-function communication, then it should be declared as a *static* variable. The scope of global static variables is restricted to the file containing them which prevents functions in other files from accessing these variables.

Storage for an external variable can be allocated only in one module. The definition of an external variable is just like its declaration, but it does not use the keyword *extern*. An external variable definition must be given outside a function body.

Several files can reference the same external variable, by giving identical declarations (one file must contain a matching definition for the external variable), allowing functions to communicate with each other by reading and updating these external variables. External variables represent one of the two primary mechanisms in C for inter-function communication, the other being function arguments (see Chapter 5 for more details).

Here is the *main* function (stored in file *double.c*):

```
#include "double.h"
int line_no = 1;

main()
{
  char next[WL+1], last[WL+1];

  last[0] = '\0';
  while ((word(next)) != EOF) {
    if (strcmp(next, last) == 0)
      printf("double word **%s** on line %d\n",
                                    last, line_no);
    strcpy(last, next);
  }
}
```

We have seen the *#include* statement several times before. However, this is the first time that it has been used to include a user-defined file. The file to be included, *double.h*, is enclosed in double quotes instead of angle brackets as done in the earlier *#include* instructions. The only difference between the use of angle brackets and double quotes is that in case of names enclosed in double quotes, the C preprocessor looks in the current directory before looking in the standard places where it expects to find the files. Of course, in either case (whether angle brackets or double quotes are used), if an absolute path name is specified, as in

```
#include "\pc\driver\laser.h"
```

then there is no need to search directories.

A file inclusion capability is important for program modularization. Common declarations can be kept in one file and program modules that need the declarations can include the declarations file. This way the declarations do not need to be typed again for every module. Including a declarations file also ensures that every module has exactly the same declarations avoiding possible errors.

The next line is the definition of the external variable *line_no* whose declaration we saw in the header file *double.h*. A definition can be preceded by a declaration although the declaration will be redundant and not really necessary. However, a redundant declaration can help ensure that the definition matches the declaration which is what is given in the other modules. In our case, the declaration of *line_no* was included by including the header file *double.h*. This file was included for the other declarations contained in it which are required by *main*.

After the definition of *line_no* is the definition of function *main*. The variable definition statement inside function *main* defines two character arrays, *next* and *last*, both of size $WL+1$. Array subscripts start with 0, so each of the above arrays will have subscripts ranging from 0 to *WL*. These arrays will be used to hold words from the input document. As in Pascal, character arrays are used in C to implement strings. By convention, every string in C is terminated by the null character "\0"; the length of the string does not take the null character into account. Consequently, strings whose length does not exceed *WL* can be stored in these arrays.*

Array elements are referenced using one pair of square brackets for each subscript. For example, the statement

```
last[0] = '\0';
```

assigns the null character to the first element of array *last* which, according to C convention, means that *last* contains the null string.

After the above assignment statement, there is a *while* loop whose expression contains a call to the user-defined function *word*.

Function *word* stores the next word from the input file in the array argument *next* and it then returns the word length as its result. If *word* encounters the end of file, then it returns the constant *EOF* (−1).

The body of the *while* loop contains calls to two string functions, *strcmp* and *strcpy*, which are part of the standard C library. *strcmp* compares its two arguments, which must be strings, and returns −1, 0 or 1 depending upon whether its first argument is lexically less than, equal to, or greater than its second argument. *strcpy* copies its second argument to the first one. These functions are necessary because, unlike Pascal, string (array) comparison and assignment are not built into C.

One final comment about the above *main* function: the *printf* function prints a string (its first argument), the string variable *last*, and the integer variable *line_no*. The latter two are printed according to format specifiers embedded within the first argument. Strings are printed using the format specifier "%s" and integers are printed using the format specifier "%d". The format

---

* Both the Pascal and C versions of the double-word checker program use arrays of the same size (i.e., 81) to hold words. However, because Pascal programs normally do not use the C convention of terminating strings with a null character, the Pascal program can handle words of length at most 81 while the C program handles words of length at most 80.

specifiers also implicitly specify the position where the corresponding arguments will be printed within the string specified as the first argument.

Here is the definition of function *word* (stored in *word.c*):

```
#include <ctype.h>
#include "double.h"

int word(s) /*returns length of s, or EOF*/
  char s[];
{
  int c, i = 0;

  while ((c = getchar()) != EOF) {
    if (isspace(c)) {
      if (c == '\n') line_no++;
      if (i == 0)   /*skip leading white space*/
          continue;
      s[i] = '\0';  /*end of word*/
      return i-1;
    }
        s[i++] = c;
  }
  return EOF;
}
```

word is a user-defined function that returns, as its result, an integer value. The function result is specified with the *return* statement. Interesting things to note in this function are that the newline character "\n" can be compared with any other character (because "\n" is just a character, e.g., like "a"). The effect of the *continue* statement in the *while* loop is to skip execution of the remaining part of the current loop iteration and go on to the next iteration. Notice the use of the increment expression "i++" to specify the subscript of array *s*. The value of this expression is the original value of variable *i*, but as a side effect of evaluating this expression, the value of *i* is incremented by one.

Each of the above two C files was compiled separately by using the following commands:

```
lc double
lc word
```

They were then linked together with each other and with the standard C library using the MS-DOS *link* command

```
link \lc\s\c+double+word,double,double/m,\lc\s\lc
```

See your compiler reference manual for details on how to compile files, and then link together the object files produced to construct an executable file.

Some systems provide a better user interface for preparing executable programs. For example, on the UNIX system, the single command

```
cc -o double double.c word.c
```

will compile the two source files, link them, and produce an executable file named *double*.

3.4.1 DIFFERENCES BETWEEN THE PASCAL & C PROGRAMS. Comparing the Pascal and C versions of the double-word checker program, we notice the following differences:

1. A serious disadvantage of standard Pascal is that, unlike C, it does not support external (independent) compilation. This means that the whole Pascal program must be compiled as a single unit and that a small change to the Pascal program will require recompiling the whole Pascal program. Some Pascal compilers support external compilation but this is non standard.

2. The Pascal program is harder to read because the Pascal function *word* is embedded within the program *double_word* which separates the main program variable declarations from their use in the program body.

3. String processing is easy in C because of the convention that each string is terminated by the null character. For example, in C, a string is "cleared" by simply setting its first element to the null character. On the other hand, in Pascal the string must be set to blanks to "clear" its old value. This is done by setting each element of the string array to a blank.

4. In Pascal, array assignment is used for copying strings. In C, function *strcpy* is used to copy strings (C does not support array assignment).

5. Printing strings is clumsy in Pascal. Each element of the array that stores the string must be printed explicitly. In C, the output routine *printf* provides the format specifier "%s" for printing strings and, in addition, there are other functions just for printing strings, e.g., *puts*. C also has functions for reading strings.

6. C functions return a value by means of the *return* statement while Pascal functions return the value assigned to the function identifier.

7. There are no procedures as such in C. The counterpart of a Pascal procedure is a function of type *void*, i.e., a function that does not return a value.

8. A C function terminates when the *return* statement is executed or when it completes execution of its function body. In Pascal, a function or procedure terminates execution only by completing execution of its body. The lack of a facility similar to the *return* statement means that

Pascal programs must be structured such that control is transferred to the end of function (procedure) body when the work of the function (procedure) is done. This often requires the use of extra boolean variables, *if* statements or *goto* statements.

9. Unlike C, Pascal does not allow variables to be initialized in their definitions. They must be initialized explicitly by means of assignment statements. A variable initialization facility can be more efficient, e.g., the C compiler performs initialization of some classes of variables at compile time. An explicit variable initialization facility can also improve program readability.

4. FINAL COMMENTS

The objective of this chapter was to familiarize you with some basic C concepts, with C programming style, and to show you some differences between Pascal and C. The differences between the two languages lead to different programming styles for the two languages. In terms of functionality, it is important to note that you can write the same programs in Pascal (with the help of extensions provided by compilers) that you can write in C and vice versa. However, some programs may be convenient to write in one language but not in the other. With C you can write programs that are portable, modular, flexible, and efficient to implement. In this chapter, we looked at C from a high-level perspective. In subsequent chapters, we will take a closer, more detailed, look at C.

5. EXERCISES

1. Compile, link, and execute the example C programs on your computer.

2. What will be the effect of nesting comments if a C compiler does not allow nested comments?

3. Suppose you erroneously use the assignment operator "=" instead of the equality operator "= =" as in the following *if* statement:

    ```
    if (opr = '+')
        statement
    ```

    Explain the consequences of your mistake.

    Note that it is not possible to make a similar mistake in Pascal; the use of ":=" in place of "=" is detected by the compiler because assignment is not allowed in expressions.

4. Rewrite the C version of the calculator program in which the *if* statement and the nested *switch* statement are combined into just one *switch* statement that uses the *default* alternative (see Chapter 4 for more details about the *switch* statement).

5. The double-word checker does not catch double phrases such as

   `that book that book`

   Extend the double-word program to handle two-word phrases. Note that you only have to modify the *main* function (and not function *word*).

CHAPTER 2

TYPES & VARIABLES

One of the most important facilities of a programming language is its typing mechanism. Pascal and C have similar types but there is one important difference between these two languages: their type philosophies. In this chapter, we shall discuss the type philosophies of Pascal and C, the types in the two languages, type conversions, and variable declarations and definitions.

1. TYPE PHILOSOPHY

Pascal and C differ in the degree of discipline (or inflexibility, depending upon your point of view) imposed upon the programmer in manipulating objects vis-a-vis their types. Pascal is what is called a "strongly typed" language. It was the first language to popularize the notion of *strong typing*, that is, an object *must* be used in a manner that is consistent with respect to its type. Strong typing allows many errors to be detected at compile time. Without strong typing, the burden of detecting these errors falls on the programmer; the compiler cannot detect them because it does not have enough information. Despite its desirability, strong typing can be stifling for the programmer, especially the experienced or professional programmer, if it is not accompanied by convenient facilities to bypass strong typing. For example, because of strong typing, in standard Pascal it is not possible to write a general purpose storage allocator for allocating storage for different types of objects. To be more specific, it is not possible for a programmer to write a procedure with semantics similar to that of the built-in function *new*. Such a procedure must be able to accept arguments of different types, in this case pointers of different types, as accepted by *new*.

C is typed language, but it is not as strongly typed as Pascal. C gives the programmer many of the benefits of strong typing without preventing the programmer from bypassing the typing mechanism. For instance, writing a storage allocator in C equivalent to the one mentioned above is straightforward. A programmer just writes a function that allocates the specified storage and then returns a pointer, say a character pointer, to this storage. This pointer is "cast" (converted) to the desired type, if necessary, by the programmer. In C, any "fundamental" (basic or primitive) type can be converted to any other fundamental type. Similarly, any pointer type can

31

be converted to any other pointer type. Because Pascal does not allow such type conversions, it is not possible to write a general purpose storage allocator in standard Pascal.

with a few exceptions, Pascal and C have similar types. C does not have an explicit boolean type (integer types are used as substitutes), and it does not have the subrange and the set types. But, unlike Pascal, C provides several integer and real types of different sizes.

The two languages use different terminologies for classifying types. The fundamental types of C are the counterparts of the simple types (scalar types and reals) in Pascal. The derived types of C correspond to the structured and the pointer types of Pascal.

2. CONSTANTS & CONSTANT DEFINITIONS

2.1 CONSTANTS (LITERALS)

C provides facilities for specifying constants of type (single precision) integer, long (double precision) integer, (double precision) floating point, character, enumeration, and string.

Octal and hexadecimal integer constants can also be specified in C. Octal constants are specified with a leading 0 (as in 022), and hexadecimal constants are specified with a leading 0x or 0X as in 0x5A.

The letter l (or L) at the end of an integer constant specifies that it is a long integer (or simply long) constant. All floating point constants are interpreted as double precision constants. The letter e (or E) is used to specify the exponent of floating point constants written in the scientific notation, for example, 3.198e2 (i.e., 319.8).

C string constants are specified by enclosing a sequence of characters within double quotes (Pascal uses single quotes). Character constants are denoted by enclosing the specified character in single quotes, for example, 'c', 'A', '\n', and '\033' (use of the backslash character to specify special characters is discussed below).

Pascal does not distinguish between characters and strings. Characters are just strings of length one. C characters are not the same as one-character strings. This is because in C strings are sequences of characters terminated by the null character which is denoted as "\0". For example, the string "a" actually consists of two characters: the letter *a* and the null character. By convention the null character is not counted in the string length.

C also provides a special denotation for some non-printing characters and some special characters:

\\	(backslash)
\n	(newline)
\t	(horizontal tab)
\v	(vertical tab)
\f	(form feed)
\r	(carriage return)
\0	(null character)
\'	(single quote)
\"	(double quote)

The backslash character is used to suppress the special role played by some characters in C. For example, to include the double quote character in a string, the denotation "\"" is used. The alternative denotations of the single and double quote characters with the preceding backslash allow them to be treated as ordinary characters and not as delimiters.

In addition, any ASCII character can be denoted as "*ddd*" where *ddd* stands for one to three octal digits specifying the ASCII encoding of the character (see Appendix 2). This notation is used especially for specifying control characters and other non-printing characters. For instance, the escape character *esc* is denoted as "\033".

Most C compilers store characters internally as integer values corresponding to their ASCII encoding. C programmers often exploit this information when manipulating characters. For example, knowledge of the ASCII encoding can be used to efficiently convert lower-case characters to upper-case characters and vice versa. If c is a lower-case character, then the expression

```
c + 'A' - 'a'
```

denotes the ASCII encoding of the upper-case character corresponding to c.

2.2 SYMBOLIC CONSTANTS

Like Pascal, C provides a facility for defining symbolic constants. Constants are given symbolic names by using the C preprocessor *#define* instruction which has the form

```
#define name constant
```

The # character must appear in column one. The *#define* instruction shown here is a special case of the more general form allowed by the C preprocessor. See Chapter 7 for more details.

Here are some examples of constant definitions:

```
#define MAX 132
#define WORD_SIZE 4
#define TRUE  1
#define FALSE 0
#define NULL  0
#define EOF (-1)
```

Symbolic names can enhance program readability and can make it easier to modify and maintain programs. If the value of a symbolic constant is to be changed, for example, then only the constant definition will need to be changed and not all uses of the constant.

3. FUNDAMENTAL (SIMPLE) TYPES

C provides the following fundamental types: void, character, integer, floating point, and enumeration types. Character and integer types are collectively called the *integral* types; integral and floating point types are collectively called the *arithmetic* types.

3.1 VOID

C has functions but no procedures. Procedures are functions that do not return any values. Such functions are defined in C by specifying that their result type to be the *void* (empty) type. No values or operations are associated with the *void* type. It is used primarily to indicate that a function will not return a result. Note that there is no need for the *void* type in Pascal, since Pascal has both functions and procedures.

As examples illustrating the use of the *void* type, consider the following declaration of function *swapi** and the definition of function *error*:

```
void swapi();

void error(msg)
    char *msg;
{
    printf("Error: %s\n", msg);
    exit(1);
}
```

Not all C compilers support the *void* type because it is a recent addition to the C language [Harb84]. The *void* type is not specified in K&R C, but its inclusion in ANSI C is likely. The *void* type does not extend the functionality

---

*   A declaration should be given for a function if it will be referenced before its definition is encountered. The function may be given later in the same file or it may be contained in a separate file.

of C, but it does allow C compilers to perform better type checking and it improves program readability.

Porting programs to a C compiler that does not support the *void* type is straightforward; just define *void* to be a synonym for *int*:

```
#define void int
```

Functions declared as *void* will now return an integer value. However, the value returned will be garbage, because no return value will be explicitly specified in the function body. The garbage return value is of no consequence if it is not used: the value will simply be discarded.

3.2 INTEGERS

Pascal has only one integer type, *integer*, but it allows the user to define new integer types whose values are a subset (subrange) of *integer*. C, on the other hand, has three integer types denoted as *int*, *short*, and *long*. As mentioned earlier, C does not have a facility for defining subrange types. The subrange facility allows the Pascal programmer to define a large number of integer types whose values are a subset of the predefined integer type. However, the subrange type facility cannot be used to define integer types that have a greater precision than the predefined integer type.

Types *short* (or *short int*) and *long* (or *long int*) are variations of type *int* which respectively offer less and more precision than type *int*. Due to the difference in precision, *short* and *long* variables respectively require less and more storage than variables of type *int*. Type *int* is usually mapped to the natural word size of the machine.

Some compilers may treat *short* as a synonym for *int* offering no saving of storage or difference in precision. Similarly, other compilers may treat *long* as a synonym for *int*. However, most compilers do provide at least two flavors of integers, that is, they do not treat both *short* and *long* to be synonyms of type *int*. On the IBM PC, C compilers (including the Lattice C compiler) typically treat *short* as a synonym for *int* implementing both *short* and *int* using one word of memory. But type *long* is treated differently from *int* and is implemented using two words.

Integers of the types discussed above are called *signed* integers. If the representation of an integer (the way an integer is stored in a computer word) is to be manipulated as a bit pattern, then the integer type should be specified to be *unsigned*. In the case of *unsigned* integers the sign bit is not treated as a special bit. This means that unsigned integers can be used to hold larger positive integers.

Here are some examples of integer variable definitions and function declarations:

```
int i;
short a = 0, b = -1;
long p;
unsigned word;   /*same as unsigned int*/
int getchar(), scanf();
```

The last line is a declaration because it does not cause any storage to be allocated. It states that functions *getchar* and *scanf*, which will be used in the program, return an integer value.

3.3 FLOATING POINT (REAL) TYPES

Pascal has one floating point type while C has two floating point types: a single precision floating point type called *float* and a double precision floating point type called *double*. All *float* values are converted to *double* before performing an operation (and, if necessary, converted back to *float* after the operation). In this sense, *float* is not a full-fledged type. However, ANSI C intends to make *float* a full-fledged type. In K&R C, the main reason for using *float* is to save storage; however, the use of *float* does slow program execution due to the conversions to *double* required when operating on *float* values.

Here are some examples of floating point variable definitions:

```
float f;
double a, b;
```

3.4 ENUMERATIONS

Like Pascal, C has enumeration types. Here is an example of an enumeration type declaration and an enumeration variable definition in C:

```
enum day {sun, mon, tue, wed, thu, fri, sat};
enum day d;
```

The identifier *day* is called the enumeration tag. Because of the presence of the keyword *enum*, enumeration type variable definitions that use enumeration tags do not look quite the same as definitions involving fundamental types such as *int*. However, enumeration types declared using the recently added *typedef* facility do not have this problem. For instance, type *day* and variable *d* could alternatively have been declared and defined respectively as

```
typedef enum {
    sun, mon, tue, wed, thu, fri, sat
} day;
day d;
```

Variable *d* can be assigned values of type *day* as in the assignment

```
d = sun;
```

Here is an example illustrating the use of the above enumeration variable:

```
if (d == sun || d == sat)
    total_pay += daily_wage * 1.5;
else
    total_pay += daily_wage;
```

The above statement could have been written alternatively as

```
total_pay+=daily_wage*((d==sun||d==sat)?1.5:1);
```

Note that a statement of the form

a += b;

is equivalent to the statement

a = a + b;

provided the evaluation of *a* causes no side effects. Also the conditional expression

a?b:c

evaluates to *b* if *a* is non-zero and to *c* otherwise.

Enumeration types, like the *void* type, have been recently added to C [Harb84]. Because the enumeration type is not part of K&R C, not all compilers implement it, and those that do, do not implement it consistently. Most C compilers implementing enumeration types treat them as integers. Some C compilers issue warnings when an enumeration type is treated as an integer by the programmer, for example, when an integer value is assigned to an enumeration type variable, but this is not much in the way of error protection. Note that the Lattice C compiler does not allow enumeration types to be treated as integers and vice versa.

By default, most compilers assign zero to the first enumeration constant, one to the second enumeration constant, and so on. The following example, which exploits the above information, illustrates how to iterate through all elements of an enumeration type in C:

```
enum day {sun, mon, tues, wed, thu, fri, sat};
enum day d[7];
int i;

for (i=0; i<6; i++)
    d[i] = (enum day) i;
            /*convert i to enumeration type day*/
            /*before the assignment*/
```

Because the C *for* loop does not automatically increment (or decrement) the loop variable, and because C does not provide the equivalent of the Pascal *succ* and *pred* functions, it is not straightforward to write a *for* loop with a loop variable of an enumeration type. Consider the Pascal loop shown below:

```
type day = (sun, mon, tue, wed, thu, fir, sat);
var d: day;
...
for d := sun to sat do ...
```

To write an equivalent loop, two type conversions are necessary: one to convert the enumeration type loop variable to an integer so that it can be incremented, and the second to convert the integer back to the enumeration type:

```
enum day {sun, mon, tues, wed, thu, fri, sat};
enum day d;
...
for (d=sun; d<sat; d=(enum day) ((int) d+1)) ...
```

3.5 CHARACTERS

Like the Pascal character type, the C character type is denoted by the identifier *char*. However, the C *char* type is not an enumeration type like the Pascal *char* type. Here are some example definitions of character variables in C:

```
char a;
char c, delim = ':';
```

C provides many functions for classifying character values; for example, there are functions to determine if a character is alphabetic, numeric, alphanumeric, or printable. Functions for character conversion, such as those for converting characters from one case to another, are also provided. Details of these functions are given in Appendix 1.

An important difference between the Pascal and C character types is that in C characters are stored and treated as integers. The internal value of a character is its encoding in the underlying character set, e.g., ASCII (see Appendix 2). This internal representation of a character is visible to the programmer. Consequently, there is no need in C for the Pascal functions *chr* and *ord*. For example, the following assignment stores the character with ASCII encoding 7 (the *bel* character) in the character or integer variable *a*:

```
a = 7;
```

Similarly, to print the integer representation of a character, the character is printed as if it were an integer.

Mixing integers and characters is a common C paradigm. In fact, C programmers treat *char* variables as very small (8-bit) integers. Integers, such as negative integers, that are not valid encodings of characters should not be stored in *char* variables; otherwise, the result may be undefined. If a character variable occasionally has to store an integer that is not a valid character encoding, or if a function that normally returns characters occasionally returns such an integer, then they should be defined to be of an integer type and not of type *char*. For example, the C function *getchar* normally returns the next character from the standard input, but it returns the integer constant *EOF* (–1) to indicate the end of file. Consequently, *getchar* is defined a function that returns an integer (*int*) value.

3.6 BOOLEANS

C does not have a boolean type. C treats a non-zero value as true and zero as false. By convention, the built-in comparison operators return one, instead of an arbitrary non-zero value, to indicate true. Because C does not have an explicit boolean type, C compilers cannot catch errors that are routinely caught by Pascal compilers. For example, the expression

$a < b < c$

where a, b, and c are integers, is flagged as error in Pascal but not in C. This is because in Pascal the result of comparing two values is a boolean value and a boolean value cannot be compared with an integer value. Although the above expression is legal in C because the result of comparing two numbers is an integer, writing such an expression can give an incorrect result. Fortuitously, the expression

$1 < 2 < 3$

correctly evaluates to 1 (true) in C (assuming a left-to-right order of evaluation). But the expression

$1 < 99 < 3$

also, and this time incorrectly, evaluates to 1 (again assuming left-to-right order of evaluation). Although expressions of the form shown above are commonly used in mathematics, they are not allowed in most programming languages. Such expressions must be written using the logical *and* operator (&& in C):

$a < b$ && $b < c$

3.7 SUBRANGES

C does not have a facility corresponding to the Pascal subrange type.

4. DERIVED (STRUCTURED & POINTER) TYPES

Derived types are types constructed using fundamental types and previously declared derived types. Derived types that can be constructed in C are arrays, structures, unions, and pointers. As mentioned earlier, unlike Pascal, C does not have the set type.

4.1 ARRAYS

Arrays in Pascal and C are conceptually quite similar, but there are several differences:

1. Unlike Pascal, C (compilers) does not do array subscript checking. It is the responsibility of the programmer to ensure that an out-of-bounds subscript will not be used. If an out-of-bounds subscript is used, then it will refer to a memory location outside the array. The program will terminate if the memory location is in a region protected by the underlying operating system.

2. In addition to integer subscripts, Pascal arrays can have enumeration (which includes character and boolean) values as subscripts. C arrays can have only integer subscripts.

3. Pascal arrays can have any lower and upper bounds (including negative integers) provided the upper bound is greater than or equal to the lower bound. The lower bound in case of a C array is always 0.

4. Pascal supports array assignment but C does not.

5. ISO Pascal supports the notion of "conformant arrays" which allows subprograms to accept arrays of different sizes, in different subprogram calls, as arguments corresponding to the same parameter. ANSI Pascal and J&W Pascal do not support conformant arrays. C functions can accept arrays of different sizes.

6. In Pascal, but not in C, the user can instruct the compiler to pack the array as compactly as possible.

7. Global ("external" and "file static") C arrays can be initialized in their definitions. Such array initialization is not allowed in Pascal. When an array with explicitly specified initial element values is defined in C, then the size of the first dimension need not be given: the C compiler determines the size of the missing array dimension by counting the number of initial values.

8. Pascal does not support dynamic arrays—arrays whose dimensions are specified by arbitrary expressions. Such arrays can be defined in C because of the special relationship between arrays and pointers (see Chapter 6). Dynamic arrays allow C programmers to define arrays of exactly the size needed for the program. In Pascal, array sizes are static and the programmer must declare arrays that are large enough to handle all possible cases even though, in most cases, smaller size arrays would have been appropriate. Use of larger than necessary arrays wastes storage which can be a critical resource in some applications.

9. C arrays are not full-fledged objects like objects of other derived types such as pointers and structures (both are discussed later). For example, array assignment is not allowed while pointer and structure assignment is allowed.

As an example of C arrays, consider the following definitions of arrays:

```
int a[10], b[25][5], c[5][5][5];
```

a, *b*, and *c* are defined to be one-, two-, and three-dimensional arrays, respectively. Notice that a pair of square brackets is required for each array dimension.

The C notation for referencing array elements is similar to the Pascal notation with one exception: each subscript *must* be enclosed in square bracket pairs as in

```
a[i]
b[i]
b[i][j]
c[i][j][k]
```

4.1.1 COUNTING CHARACTERS EXAMPLE. We will write a program that reads characters from standard input and counts the number of times the various letters occur in the input. No distinction will be made between lower- and upper-case letters. Array *ct* will be used to store the letter counts: element *f[c-'a']* will store the number of times letter *c* appears in the input. (All C arrays begin with the subscript zero. Had it been possible to specify alternative first subscripts, for example, that the first subscript of *ct* be the ASCII encoding of the letter "a", then the number of times letter *c* appears in the input would have been stored in element *ct[c]*.)

Here is the C program that counts the number of times letters appear in its input (stored in file *freq.c*):

```
#include <stdio.h>
#include <ctype.h>

#define NO_LET 26

int ct[NO_LET];   /*external variables are */
                  /*initialized to zero, by*/
                  /*default*/
main()
{
    int c, i;

    while ((c = getchar()) != EOF)
        if (isalpha(c)) {
            c = tolower(c);   /*convert to lower*/
            ct[c-'a']++;
        }
    for (i=0; i < NO_LET; i++)
        printf("%c count = %d\n",i+'a',ct[i]);
}
```

Note that input redirection can be used to count the number of times letters appear in any file.

4.1.2 VECTOR ADDITION EXAMPLE. Here is a function that adds two integer vectors (one-dimensional arrays) and puts their result in a third:

```
void vadd(a, b, c, n)
    int a[], b[], c[], n;
{
    int i;

    for (i = 0; i < n; i++)
        c[i] = b[i] + a[i];
}
```

The *void* (empty) type specifies that function *vadd* does not return any value; that is, *vadd* is for all practical purposes a procedure. Notice that array dimensions are not specified in the declarations of parameters *a*, *b*, and *c*. Function *vadd* assumes that each of the three arrays has at least *n* elements. When calling a function with array arguments, it is often necessary to pass their sizes as additional arguments.

A similar function that adds arrays of different sizes can only be written in ISO Pascal but not in J&W Pascal nor in ANSI Pascal. This is because in J&W Pascal and in ANSI Pascal the bounds of each dimension of an array parameter are specified in the parameter declaration and the corresponding array argument must have the same bounds. In fact, an array parameter and the corresponding array argument must both be of the same user-defined type.

4.1.3 BINARY SEARCH EXAMPLE. We will conclude this section on arrays with one final example. With a sorted array, the *binary search* technique can be used to locate the index of an array element with a specific value. The binary search technique first examines the middle element of the array to see if it is equal to the search value. If yes, then the search is complete. Otherwise, if the search value is less than the middle element, then the upper portion of the array is "binary searched"; if the search value is more than the middle element, then the bottom portion of the array is "binary searched" (this assumes that the array elements are sorted in increasing order). On the average, binary search is much faster than sequential search; this difference becomes more noticeable as the array size increases.

Here is function *search* that implements binary search (stored in file *search.c*):

```
/*search sorted array a for value x; return*/
/*k such that a[k]==x; otherwise, return -1*/

int search(a, n, x)
    int a[], n, x;
{
    int l = 0, u = n-1, k;

    while (l <= u)
        if (a[k = (l+u)/2] == x)
            return k;
        else if (a[k]<x)
            l = k+1;
        else
            u = k-1;
    return -1;
}
```

Notice the use of the assignment operator in the array subscript expression, within the *if* expression, to compute the midpoint *k* of the array. Had the assignment to *k* been done before the *if* statement, as would be done in languages like Pascal in which assignment is not an operator, then the *while* loop in the above program would have been written as

```
while (l <= u) {
    k = (l+u)/2;
    if (a[k] == x)
        return k;
    else if (a[k]<x)
        l = k+1;
    else
        u = k-1;
}
```

4.2 STRUCTURES (RECORDS)

Records are called structures in C. Pascal records without variant parts are the counterparts of C structures. The C union type corresponds to the variant part of a Pascal record (without the tag field). A full-fledged Pascal record with a variant part can be implemented in C by using structures and unions. Unions are discussed in the next section.

A C structure type has the form

```
struct tag {
    structure component declarations
}
```

The structure tag, which gives a symbolic name to a structure, is optional.

Structure types can be used like other types to define and declare identifiers. Here are some examples (without structure tags):

```
struct {
    char *name;   /*pointer to name*/
    int id, age, sex;
    char *mngr_name;
} a, emp[MAX], *p;

struct {double x, y;} p1, p2;
```

Structure tags are similar to enumeration tags. Here are some examples illustrating the use of structure tags:

```
struct employee {
    char *name;
    int id, age, sex;
    char *mngr_name;
};
struct coordinate {double x, y;};

struct employee a, emp[MAX], *p;
struct coordinate p1, p2;
```

The keyword *struct* must be used when using structure tags to define or declare variables or functions. However, this keyword is not used when using structure type names declared with the C type definition facility *typedef*. As mentioned earlier, the *typedef* mechanism is a recent addition to the C language and, in a sense, it duplicates the structure tag mechanism making it almost redundant. However, as shown later, structure tags are still necessary for defining recursive structures.

Here are some examples of structure type names specified with the *typedef* facility and examples illustrating their use:

```
typedef struct {
    char make[N], model[N];
    int year;
    float cc, hp;
} automobile;

typedef struct {
    double r, i;
} complex;

automobile a, b;
complex c, d;
```

Structure type names, rather than structure tags, are more like the predefined type names such as *int* and *double*.

Like Pascal, C supports structure assignment (old C compilers may not), allows structures to be given as arguments in function calls and structures can be returned as function results. However, in C but not in Pascal, global structure variables (that is, external or file static variables which are discussed later) can be given initial values in their definitions.

4.2.1 REFERENCING STRUCTURE COMPONENTS. Structure components are referenced, as in Pascal, using the selected component notation which has the form

structure-name . component-name

Here are some examples of structure components (using the variable definitions given above):

```
c.x
c.y
a.make
(*p).name
```

C provides an alternative notation for referencing structure components using a pointer to the structure. Using this notation, the last example shown above can be written alternatively as

```
p->name
```

C does not have a counterpart of the Pascal *with* statement which allows record components to be accessed conveniently and efficiently.

4.2.2 RECURSIVE STRUCTURES. As mentioned above, the *typedef* mechanism has not completely eliminated the need for structure tags. They are still necessary for defining a recursive structure such as

```
struct student {
    char first, last[MAX];
    int id;
    float gpa;
    struct student *next;
};
```

Even if the *typedef* declaration had been used, a structure tag would still be necessary:

```
typedef struct student {
    char first, last[MAX];
    int id;
    float gpa;
    struct student *next;
} student;
```

The same name, *student* in the above example, can be used for both the structure tag and the type name because structure tags and type names occupy different "name spaces".

4.2.3 EXAMPLE ILLUSTRATING USE OF STRUCTURES. The following pair of functions add and multiply values of the structure type *complex* (stored in file *complex.c*):

```
#include "complex.h"

complex add(a, b)
    complex a, b;
{
    complex c;
    c.r = a.r+b.r;
    c.i = a.i+b.i;
    return c;
}

complex mul(a, b)
    complex a, b;
{
    complex c;
    c.r = a.r*b.r - a.i*b.i;
    c.i = a.r+b.i + a.i*b.r;
    return c;
}
```

File *complex.h* contains the declaration of the type *complex* which is declared as shown earlier, that is,

```
typedef struct {
    double r, i;
} complex;
```

Here are some examples illustrating the use of the *complex* functions shown above:

```
complex x, y, z;
  ...
z = add(x, mul(y, z));
```

4.3 UNIONS (VARIANT RECORDS)

The variant part of a Pascal record is used to specify record components that may be different for different variables of the same record type. Each instance can have only one variant component which allows the compiler to "overlay" the different variant components on the same storage.

A C structure cannot have variant parts but C does provide another type called the *union* which is like the variant part of a Pascal record. Like variant components, the union components are allocated on the same storage area. This allows a storage area to be interpreted, in multiple ways, according to the types of the union components. Unlike variant records in Pascal, no "variant tag" (variant selector) variable is included in the union type to indicate the active component. It is the responsibility of the programmer to define and maintain such a selector variable.

Unions are similar to structures with regard to definitions, declarations, and component selection. The main difference is that all the union components, unlike structure components, are mapped to the same storage. Here is what a union type looks like:

```
union tag {
      component₁;
      component₂;
      ...
      componentₙ;
}
```

The union tag, like the structure tag, is optional and is used to give a symbolic name to a union type. Note that union tags are type names and are not variables corresponding to the variant tag fields in Pascal records.

As an example of storage overlay using unions, consider the union named *point*, given below, which allows the position of a point to be specified either in terms of cartesian or polar coordinates:

```
union {
      struct {double x, y;} cartesian;
      struct {double r, theta;} polar;
} point;
```

Components of this union are accessed as

```
point.cartesian.x
point.cartesian.y
point.polar.r
point.polar.theta
```

The value stored in *point* will either be in cartesian coordinates or in polar coordinates. In the first case the *cartesian* component structure will be used to access or update this value while in the second case the *polar* component structure will be used. Another variable, say *kind*, must be used to note the type of coordinates currently being stored in union *point*. Uses of the value of variable *point* must be based on the value of the "indicator" variable *kind*. For example,

```
switch (kind) {
case 0: use the cartesian structure of union point;
case 1: use the polar structure of union point;
}
```

4.3.1 IMPLEMENTING PASCAL VARIANT RECORDS IN C. Implementing Pascal variant records in C requires using a structure with a nested union and a component that indicates the active union component. For example, consider the following Pascal variant record type *geom_figure*:

```
type geom_figure =
  record
    area: real;
    case shape: (circle,triangle,square,point) of
    circle: (r: real);
    triangle: (a, b, c: real);
    square: (l, w: real);
    point: ();
  end
```

This variant record type can be implemented in C as

```
typedef struct {
    float area;
    enum {CIRCLE, TRIANGLE, SQUARE, POINT} shape;
    union {
        struct {float r;} circle;
        struct {float a, b, c;} triangle;
        struct {float l, w;} point;
    } figure;
} geom_figure;
```

The notation for referencing components of the above "variant structure" type is not as elegant as the notation used for accessing components of Pascal variant records. For example, suppose *g* is a variable of type *geom_figure*. Then element *a* of the *triangle* variant is referenced in Pascal as *g.a* while in C it will be referenced as *g.figure.triangle.a*. If element *a* is to be referenced often, then it may be more convenient and more efficient to store its address in a pointer variable, say *pa*, and then use this pointer to refer to *a*:

```
float *pa = &g.figure.triangle.a;
    /*stores address of union element a*/
    /*in pointer pa*/
...
*pa = *pa/2 + 5.0;
```

Note that the first component of the above union is a structure that contains only one element, i.e., *r*. A structure was used because otherwise the notation used for referencing *r* would be different from that used for referencing elements of the other variant components.

4.4 POINTERS

A *pointer* value refers to a specific location in memory. C pointers are similar to Pascal pointers except that they are much more flexible. Pascal pointers can refer only to dynamically allocated objects while C pointers can also refer to the address of a variable, a function, or a block of storage. In Pascal, the only operations allowed on pointer values are assignment and comparison. In addition to these operations, C also allows pointer arithmetic, conversions between pointer types, and conversions to and from pointer types.

Pointers are used in C

- for passing addresses of variables as arguments to functions to allow them to change variable values. Also, in case of large objects, passing a pointer to the object is more efficient than passing the object itself (requires less storage for the parameter and avoids copying of the object).

- to implement dynamic structures such as lists, which are more flexible and more efficient than arrays for keeping items which are frequently deleted or added.

- to read from and write to arbitrary locations in memory, subject to any constraints imposed by the operating system.

Pointers are defined and declared by using the dereferencing operator *. Here are some examples:

```
char *p;
FILE *fp;
struct {double x, y;} *pc;
int *a[10], (*b)[10];
double **pd;

char *malloc();
```

Variables *p*, *fp*, and *pc* are respectively defined as pointers of type *char*, *FILE*, and the structure given in the definition of *pc*. Variable *a* is defined as an array of integer pointers and variable *b* is defined as a pointer to an array of integers. Notice that parentheses are used in the definition of *b* to ensure that *b* is bound to the dereferencing operator * and not to the subscript operator *[]*. Variable *pd* is defined as a pointer of type pointer to a *double* object. Finally, *malloc* is declared as a function that returns a character pointer as its result.

Objects pointed to by pointers are also referenced by using the dereferencing operator *. Here are some examples which use the definitions and the function declaration given above:

p	Pointer to an integer object.
*p	The integer object pointed to by *p*.
(*pc).x	The *x* component of the structure pointed to by *pc*.
*a[i]	The integer object pointed to by the ith element of *a*.
(*b)[i]	The ith element of the array pointed to by *b*.
pd	Pointer to a pointer to a *double* value.
malloc(n)	The character pointer result returned by the function *malloc*.

Pointers are frequently used to point to structures. C provides the indirect selection operator -> for simplifying the notation used to access structure components. For example, as mentioned earlier, instead of accessing component *x* of the structure pointed to by the pointer variable *pc* as

```
(*pc).x
```

it can be accessed using -> as

```
pc->x
```

C definitions and declarations can sometimes get hard to understand. The one important thing to remember is that the notation used for defining and declaring a variable mirrors the notation used for referencing the variable. For a detailed discussion of C definitions and declarations, and how to understand complex definitions and declarations, see *C for Personal Computers* [Geha85].

Here are some examples of assignments to pointer variables:

```
char *malloc(), *s;
int *pi, i, n;
employee *p, *q;
    ...
if ((s = malloc(n)) == NULL) {...}
pi = &i;
p = q;
```

The constant identifier *NULL* denotes the null pointer; it is defined in the header file *stdio.h* as the constant zero:

```
#define NULL 0
```

The null pointer *NULL* can be assigned to a pointer variable of any type. By convention, functions that return a pointer value, such as *malloc*, return the null pointer *NULL* to indicate an error or a terminating condition.

In the assignment "*pi = &i*", the pointer variable *pi* is assigned the address of variable *i*. (The *address of* operator "*&*" extracts the address of its argument.) After this assignment *$*pi$* and *i* become synonyms for each other because both of them refer to the same integer object. The value of variable *i* can now be changed by using the pointer *pi*. For example, the assignment

```
*pi = 5;
```

changes the value of variable *i* to 5.

Similarly, after the assignment "*p = q*", *p* and *q* become synonyms for each other because they both point to the same object (of type *employee*).

As an example illustrating the use of pointers, we shall write a function to exchange the values of two integer variables. Here is a first attempt to write a function to swap integers:

```
void swapi(a, b)
    int a, b;
{
    int tmp;

    tmp = a;
    a = b;
    b = tmp;
}
```

Suppose we call *swapi* with two integer variables *x* and *y*:

```
swapi(x, y);
```

This version of *swapi* does not work. When called with two variables *x* and *y* to be swapped, *swapi* copies their values into parameters *a* and *b*, and then exchanges the values of *a* and *b*. Meanwhile, the values of variables *x* and *y* remain unchanged because all arguments are passed by value in C. C does not support passing parameters by reference; i.e., C does not support "*var*" parameters.

Pointers and variable addresses are used to simulate passing arguments by reference. For example, to make sure that the values of two integer variables are exchanged, *swapi* must be modified so that it is called with the addresses of *x* and *y*:

```
swapi(&x, &y);
```

The addresses of *x* and *y* will now be stored in the parameters *a* and *b*. Using the addresses of *x* and *y*, their values can now be changed. Here is the modified version of *swapi*:

```
void swapi(a, b)
    int *a, *b;
{
    int tmp;

    tmp = *a;
    *a = *b;
    *b = tmp;
}
```

The modified version uses the addresses in *a* and *b* to change the values of the arguments to be swapped (*x* and *y* in this example). Note that *a* contains the address of *x*; therefore, **a* is a synonym for *x*. Similarly, **b* is a synonym for *y*.

Pointers are a very important aspect of C and their use dominates many C programs. We have discussed them briefly here to give you an idea about what C pointers are like and how they are used. There is also a close and mutually beneficial relationship between pointers and arrays (and therefore strings). Pointers are discussed in more detail in Chapter 6.

4.5 SETS

Unlike Pascal, C does not have a predefined set type. But using bit manipulation operators and C preprocessor macro definitions, it is easy to define sets. See Chapter 7 for an example.

4.6 FILES

A file is a structured type in Pascal much like an array except that it must be accessed sequentially. Pascal (internal) files, i.e., objects of type *file*, are mapped to files supported by the computer system, i.e., permanent or external files. Files are not a built-in type in C, but C compilers, as part of their standard environment, provide numerous functions to manipulate permanent files. These files are referenced using "file descriptors" which are objects of the predefined file pointer type (*FILE* ∗ to be precise). C compilers provide functions for manipulating both sequential and random-access files. Because files are a built-in type in Pascal, compilers can ensure that all values written to a file are of the same type (e.g., student records). In C, it is the programmer's responsibility to ensure that all values written to a file are of the same type.

In standard Pascal, names of all permanent files that will be manipulated in the program (including standard input, standard output, and standard error, and files created by the program) must be passed as arguments to the Pascal program (these names are listed in the *program* statement). C is more flexible. File names are strings in C and this allows file names to be passed as arguments to the program, read in as data or constructed in the program itself. For more information about file manipulation, see the Section 2 titled *"INPUT/OUTPUT"* in Chapter 4 for a summary and Appendix 1 for details.

4.7 STRINGS

Like Pascal, C does not provide a predefined string type and strings are implemented as character arrays. By convention, C strings are terminated by the null character "\0". This is a very important convention that no C programmer can afford to forget. Strings *must* be terminated with the null character; otherwise, none of the library string functions will work properly and this will lead to errors. C compilers also follow this convention; they automatically add the terminating null character at the end of each string literal.

As an example illustrating string manipulation in C, consider the following code that is used to read all the characters up to the next blank from the standard input and store them in the character array *word*:

```
int c, i = 0;
char word[MAX+1];

while ((c = getchar()) != EOF)
    word[i++] = c;
word[i] = '\0';
```

Notice that the string is terminated explicitly by storing the null character at the end of the array. (Statement *"word[i++] = c;"* is equivalent to the statement *"word[i] = c;"* followed by the statement *"i=i+1;"*.) The length of the string in array *word* can be determined by calling the library function *strlen* which simply counts the characters in a string up to the null character.

Because Pascal does not use an equivalent of the C string termination convention,* an extra variable must be used to store the length of the string stored in *word*.

Because strings are not a built-in type in C, there are no built-in facilities to manipulate strings. For example, there are no built-in operators for string assignment, string concatenation, and string comparison. But as part of the standard library, C compilers provide many functions for manipulating strings.

---

* Note that there is no direct denotation for the null character in Pascal. Function *chr* must be used to specify the null character.

For example, function *strcpy* does string assignment, function *strcat* does string concatenation, and function *strcmp* does string comparison. String functions are classified into the following categories: copy, concatenation, comparison, length, and searching. See Appendix 1 for details.

One of the string functions provided by the C compiler is *strlen* which determines the length of a string. Had this function not been provided, then it could have been easily written as

```
int strlen(s)
    char s[];
{
    int i = 0;
    while (s[i++] != '\0')
        ;
    return i-1;
}
```

Function *strlen* simply counts the number of characters up to, but not including, the terminating null character. The importance of the terminating null character at the end of a string cannot be emphasized too much. In the absence of this character, the above loop will go through all of memory, examining every byte, until it finds a null character or until it references an illegal address which will cause the program to terminate.

Array names are (constant) pointers to the beginning of the storage allocated for the array. Therefore, in this example, array *s* could also have been declared as a character pointer. The declaration of the library function *strlen*, which is given in Appendix 1, declares *s* to be a character pointer, i.e.,

```
char *s;
```

and not as an array as declared in the above program.

Because of the special relationship between arrays and pointers (see Chapter 6), these two declarations are equivalent: C arrays are essentially "syntactic convenience" for pointers. Often strings are manipulated using pointers instead of arrays.

As an example of a string manipulation function written in C, consider the function *left* shown below that extracts the specified number of leftmost characters of a string and stores them in another string (stored in file *left.c*):

```
void left(s, n, d) /*set d to the leftmost n*/
                    /*characters of s*/
    char s[]; int n; char d[];
{
    int i;

    if (n > strlen(s))
        strcpy(d, s);
    else {
        for (i=0; i<n; i++)
            d[i] = s[i];
        d[i] = '\0';
    }
}
```

To extract and store the leftmost 4 characters of string *y* in string *a*, function *left* is called as

```
left(y, 4, a);
```

The algorithm implemented by *left* is simple: it first checks to see if *n* is greater than the length of *s* by using the string length function *strlen*. If *n* is greater, then *left* copies *s* into *d* by calling the string copy function *strcpy*. Otherwise, it copies the first *n* characters of *s*, one character at a time, into *d* and then inserts a terminating null character at the end of *d*.

Function *left* returns a *void* (empty) value. Consequently, a call to this function cannot be used in expressions and the function call must be used as a statement (like a Pascal procedure call). Function *left* can be easily modified to return the left substring as its value: just change the type of *left* to *char* *, allocate array *d* in the function itself instead of passing it as an argument, and return the address of *d* as the function result (stored in *leftr.c*):

```
#include <stdio.h> /*contains defn. of NULL*/

char *left(s, n) /*return pointer to string  */
                 /*that contains the leftmost*/
                 /*n characters of s*/
    char s[]; int n;
{
    int i;
    char *d, *malloc();

    if ((d = malloc(n+1)) == NULL) {
        puts("not enough heap storage");
        exit(1);
    }
    if (n > strlen(s))
        strcpy(d, s);
    else {
        for (i=0; i<n; i++)
            d[i] = s[i];
        d[i] = '\0';
    }
    return d;
}
```

Function *malloc* is used to dynamically allocate storage for the array *d*. This example makes use of the special relationship between arrays and pointers. Arrays and pointers can be used interchangeably (see Chapter 6) but unlike pointer variables, array names are constants and they cannot be assigned new values. As an example illustrating this difference, consider the following code:

```
char s[MAX+1], t[MAX+1];
int n;
...
t = left(s, n);
```

The above assignment is invalid because a new value cannot be assigned to the array name *t*. However, the string returned by *left* can be explicitly copied into the existing elements of array *t* by using the string copy function:

```
strcpy(t, left(s, n));
```

The assignment shown above would have been valid had *t* been defined as a character pointer.

4.7.1 IN CORE (MEMORY) CONVERSIONS USING STRINGS. Using function *sprintf*, formatted output can be written to a string instead of a file. Similarly, using function *sscanf*, formatted input can be read from a string instead of an input file. In fact, these two functions can be used for doing arbitrary type conversions: values are written to a string with one format and then read from the string using another format. Conversions can also be accomplished by writing to a file in one format and then reading from the file in another format. However, these conversions will be slower than those done using a string because of the higher file access time.

5. TYPE CONVERSIONS

In Pascal a programmer must supply a value of the type expected according to the program context. There are exceptions to this rule: integer values are automatically converted to floating point values and subrange values are automatically converted to their base types. Functions *round* and *trunc* are used to convert floating point values to integer values, and functions *chr* and *ord* are used for converting integers to characters and vice versa. No other conversions are allowed.

C is very liberal in the ways programmers can treat values of different types. For example, character values can be used as integer values and vice versa (there is no need for functions such as *chr* and *ord*). Integral values are automatically converted to floating point and vice versa; in the latter case, C does not specify whether floating point values will be rounded or truncated. This decision is left to the implementation (the Lattice C compiler uses rounding).

In C an expression of a fundamental or a pointer type can be converted to any fundamental or pointer type by *casting* (converting) the expression to the desired type. Casts have the form

(new-type)   *expression*

As an example, suppose that *a* is a floating point variable and *p* is an integer-pointer variable. The following expressions

```
(int) (a*a)
(char *) p
```

yield the integer equivalent of *a*a* (after truncation or rounding depending upon the implementation) and a character pointer equal to *p*, respectively. Notice that in the first case, casting involves calling a function to do the conversion while in the second case only the pointer type is changed and no conversion function is actually called.

Casting is used routinely in C programs. For example, suppose storage is to be allocated for an object of type *employee* and a pointer to the object is to be stored in variable *pe*, which is a pointer of type *employee*. Because the storage allocator *malloc* always returns a character pointer to the allocated storage, the value returned by *malloc* must be cast to an *employee* pointer before storing it in *pe*. Doing the same thing in Pascal does not require casting because the Pascal storage allocator *new* is a special procedure: it accepts, as arguments, variables of any pointer type. Standard Pascal does not allow users to write procedures that accept variables of different types. Consequently, in Pascal a user cannot write a customized version of the storage allocator *new* while in C it is straightforward to write a customized version of *malloc*.

6. TYPE DEFINITIONS (USER-DEFINED TYPES)

As mentioned earlier, a type definition mechanism, the *typedef* statement, has been recently added to C. This statement is similar to the *type* definition facility of Pascal. The *typedef* statement has the form

typedef *type type-name*

where *type* can be a type name or the description of a type.

Here are some examples of type definitions:

```
typedef unsigned word;
typedef double length;
typedef struct {int a, b;} pair;
```

Type names declared using the *typedef* mechanism can be used to define (declare) variables, just as they can be defined (declared) with the predefined types such as *int* and *double*. Here are some examples illustrating use of the above types to define variables:

```
word x, w[M];
length l1, l2;
pair *p;
```

7. VARIABLE DECLARATIONS/DEFINITIONS

As mentioned earlier, unlike Pascal and many other programming languages, C makes a distinction between variable declarations and definitions. Declarations specify identifier types but they do not allocate storage. Definitions, in addition to specifying identifier types, also cause storage to be allocated for the identifiers being defined.

Using C terminology, Pascal declarations would be called definitions. The counterpart of a C declaration in Pascal is the *forward* directive which specifies the function and procedure argument types, and the function result. The *forward* directive must be used when defining mutually recursive functions.

An object declaration is given in a C program if the object will be used before it is defined or if it is defined in another file. Pascal requires declarations to be given in a strict order. The intent of this requirement is to make the programmer define an object before using it so that the compiler can perform better type checking and to facilitate the compilation process. Note there are exceptions to this rule: the *forward* directive can be used to specify subprograms which are referenced before they are defined. Pascal implementations may also provide other directives such as an *external* directive for specifying externally compiled subprograms.

7.1 VARIABLE DEFINITIONS

C variable definitions are of the form

type   declarator-list ;

where *declarator-list* contains the items being defined (declared). Here are some examples:

```
int i;
float f, g = 0.0;
char line[128];
employee e;
```

These definitions specify

- *i* to be an *int* (integer) variable,

- *f* and *g* to be *float* (floating point) variables with *g*, initialized to 0.0,

- *line* to be a *char* (character) array of length 128, and

- *e* to be a variable of the user-defined type *employee*.

Variables can be initialized, as illustrated by the initialization of *g*, in their definitions.

Type *employee* used in the last definition is not a predefined type provided by C, but instead it is a type defined by the user with the *typedef* facility.

We will not formally explain the declarator syntax; instead, it will be illustrated by means of examples given throughout the book.

7.2 STORAGE CLASSES

In C programs, the storage class of a variable determines its lifetime and scope. There are four storage classes: external, file static, automatic, and function static. To be precise, there is another storage class called *register*, but it is really a variant of the automatic storage class. There is no explicit notion of storage classes in Pascal. All Pascal variables are automatic variables in C terminology.

The scope of an external variable is the set of files containing its definition and matching declarations, and its lifetime is the lifetime of the program. External variables are used for inter-function communication. These functions can be in the same file or in different files. External variable definitions are given outside the function body. One file must contain the definition of an external variable. Each of the other files, where this external variable is referenced, must contain a matching declaration for the external variable. External variable declarations must be preceded by the keyword *extern*. External variable definitions, however, *must not* use the keyword *extern*. Function definitions (declarations) are automatically assumed to be external definitions (declarations).

As an example, consider an external integer variable *n* that is used for inter-file inter-function communication between functions *main* and *line*. Here is the file containing the definitions of variable *n* and function *main*:

```
int n = 0;
main()
{
   ... n ... line() ...
}
```

Now here is the file that contains a matching external declaration for *n* and the definition of function *line*:

```
extern int n;
char *line()
{
   ... n ...
}
```

Had *main* and *line* been in the same file, then there would have been no need for the external declaration:

```
int n = 0;
main()
{
   ... n ... line() ...
}

char *line()
{
   ... n ...
}
```

Note that in the above examples, function *line* is called from function *main*. We have not shown you the declaration of *line*. As an exercise, write the declaration of *line* and indicate the points in the above code fragments where it should be given.

File static variables are like external variables except that their scope is restricted to the file containing their definitions. These variables are used for communication between functions in the same file. File static variable definitions are given outside a function body and must be preceded by the keyword *static*.

For example, if the variable *n* shown above is to be used just for communication between functions contained in the same file, then its scope can be restricted to the file by defining it as a static variable:

```
static int n = 0;
```

Defining *n* as a file static variable ensures that functions in other files will not be able to access or update the value of *n*.

The scope of an automatic variable is the function containing its definition and its lifetime is the lifetime of the function. By default, all variables declared inside functions have the automatic storage class. These variables are automatically allocated upon function entry and deallocated upon function exit. The compiler can be instructed to put automatic variables, if possible, in registers for fast access by preceding the variable definitions with the keyword *register*.

Function static variables are like file static variables except that they are defined inside a function and this restricts their scope to be the function body. Unlike automatic variables, function static variables are allocated once, at the beginning of the program, and they are not deallocated upon function exit. Function static variables are used to remember values across function calls.

Now here is a summary of the scope and lifetime of variables of different storage classes. The scope of an external variable is the set of files containing its definition and the corresponding declarations, the scope of a file static variable is the file containing its definition, and the scope of an automatic or a function static variable is the function containing its definition. The lifetime of external and static variables is the same as the lifetime of the program and the lifetime of automatic variables is the lifetime of the function containing them.

The different variable scopes associated with the various storage classes enables a programmer to restrict the visibility of variables and functions to those parts of the program that need to access the variables and functions. The different lifetimes allow the storage to be allocated as and when needed. In contrast to the different scopes and lifetimes that are possible for C variables, the scope of all Pascal variables is the subprogram (or main program) containing them and their lifetime is the lifetime of this subprogram (or main program).

7.3 VARIABLE DECLARATIONS

Declarations are given when an object is used before it is defined (e.g., functions) or if it is defined in another file (e.g., functions and external variables).

A function declaration must be given before the function is called in the following cases: the function definition is given after the function is referenced, the function is contained in a different file, or the function

belongs to a library. The declaration specifies the function name and the
result type which allows the compiler to allocate the right amount of storage
for the function result and make sure that the function result is used
consistently with respect to its type. Note that ANSI C will also require the
programmer to specify the parameter types (as in the Pascal *forward*
directive) which will allow the compiler to do more type checking.

As mentioned earlier, external variables are used for communication between
functions contained in different files. Each external variable is defined in one
file and declared in all the other files where it is used. External variable
declarations are like the corresponding definitions except that the external
storage class keyword *extern* is given explicitly (to indicate that it is a
declaration and not a definition) and no initial values can be given in the
declaration.

Here are two examples of declarations:

```
extern int x;
int max();
```

Note that functions are automatically assumed to have the external storage
class.

7.4 VARIABLE INITIALIZATION

Unlike Pascal variables, C variables can be initialized in their definitions by
listing their initial values in their definitions. Initialization of global variables
is done at compile time. Consequently, depending upon the amount and the
kind of initialization, C's compile-time initialization can lead to a substantial
saving in execution time when compared with the use of assignment
statements to initialize variables.

Fundamental type and pointer variables are initialized with an initializer of
the form

= *expression*

In case of *external* and *static* variables, the initializing expression must be a
constant expression.

External and static arrays and structures are initialized with one of the
following three forms of initializers:

= { *list-of-expressions* }

= { *list-of-expressions* , }

= "*sequence-of-characters*"

The second initializer form is used if a value is not given for each element of
the array or for each component of the structure; elements for which an

initial value is not given are initialized to 0. The values in the initial list are separated by commas. Each value can be a constant expression or, if appropriate, a list of constant expressions enclosed in curly braces. The third form is used when assigning a string literal to a character array.

Here are some examples of variables initialized in their definitions:

```
char delim = ':';
int i, j = 0, nb = MAX*WORD_SIZE;
int f[] = {1, 2, 3};
float y[MAX] = {1.0, 1.0,};
int x[3][2] = {{1, 2}, {3, 4}, {5, 6}};
char fmt[] = "Number of employees = %d\n";
struct {int x, y;} pair = {1, 1};
```

MAX and *WORD_SIZE* are symbolic constant names. If the size of an array is not specified, as in the case of the character array *fmt*, then its size will be computed by the C compiler by counting the number of initial values given for the array elements. Notice that character arrays can be initialized to strings.

Uninitialized static and external variables are guaranteed to start off with a zero initial value. Uninitialized automatic and register variables have garbage values: they must be initialized before they are used.

8. EXERCISES

1. Write a C equivalent of the following Pascal variant record type:

```
type coordinate =
    record
        case kind: (polar, cartesian) of
            polar: (r, theta: real);
            cartesian: (x, y: real);
    end
```

2. What is the difference between C declarations and definitions? What would you call the Pascal *forward* directive in C terminology and why?

CHAPTER 3

OPERATORS & EXPRESSIONS

1. OPERATORS

C is a language rich in operators. C has unary, binary, and even ternary operators. Moreover, C has many operators for which there are no counterparts in Pascal. Examples of such operators are the conditional expression operator, the many compound assignment operators, the *sizeof* operator, and the increment/decrement operators. The numerous C operators tend to make C programs smaller than their Pascal counterparts. It also leads to a programming style that is different from that of Pascal. For example, assignment is an operator in C but not in Pascal which means that C expressions can have embedded assignments. Indeed, such use is common practice when writing C programs. The effect of the assignment expression, in addition to doing the assignment, is to return the value assigned to the variable.

C does not provide any operators for manipulating strings. However, unlike Pascal, C provides a large number of functions for manipulating strings as components of the standard libraries that come with every C compiler. Both C and Pascal do not have an exponentiation operator. But C provides an exponentiation function, named *pow*, as part of its standard math library.

In this chapter, we will list all the C operators but we will discuss in detail only those operators that are not in Pascal or those that differ substantially from the corresponding Pascal operators.

1.1 USUAL ARITHMETIC CONVERSION RULES

C arithmetic operators automatically convert their operands, according to what are called the "usual arithmetic conversion" rules, before operating on them. These conversion rules are listed below:

1. Convert *char* and *short* operands to *int*, and *float* operands to *double* (ANSI C will not allow the latter).

2. a. If one operand type is *double*, then convert the other operand to *double*; result type is *double*.
    b. Otherwise, if one operand type is *long*, then convert the other

operand to *long*; result type is *long*.

c. Otherwise, if one operand type is *unsigned*, then convert the other operand to *unsigned*; result type is *unsigned*.

d. Otherwise, both operand types must be *int*; result type is *int*.

We shall now discuss the C operators. Remember that the "usual arithmetic conversion" rules are always applied by the arithmetic operators and these conversion rules play a part in determining the result type.

1.2 FUNCTION CALL, SUBSCRIPTING & SELECTION

Operation	Operator	Operands
function call	( )	function name and argument list
subscript	[ ]	array name and integral subscript
direct selection	.	structure or union name, and component name
indirect selection	->	pointer to structure or union + component name

C treats array subscripts (specified with square brackets) and function calls (specified with parentheses) as operators. Like other operators, the subscript and function call operators have precedence and associativity rules. In Pascal, as in most other languages, array subscripts and function calls are not considered to be operators; instead, they are considered to be part of the array or the function name.

Here are two examples each of the above operators:

```
getchar()
strlen(s)

a[5]
line[i][j+1]

d.month
e.name

pd->month
pe->name
```

As mentioned earlier, in most languages function call and subscripting are not considered to be operators. Fortunately, because C assigns the highest precedence to these operators and to the structure and union component selection operators, they and their arguments can be thought of as being part of the adjacent array, function, structure, and union names, respectively. However, when two of these operators appear adjacent to each other, then it becomes necessary to think of them as operators and use operator associativity rules to parse the expression.

Pascal does not have the counterpart of the indirect selection operator. This operator can be easily expressed in terms of the direct selection and dereferencing operators in both C and Pascal. For example, the C expression

```
pd->month
```

can alternatively be written as

```
(*pd).month
```

where * is the C dereferencing operator. The parentheses are necessary because selection has a higher precedence than dereferencing in C.

1.3 UNARY OPERATORS

Operation	Operator	Operands	Result Type	Notes
dereferencing	*	pointer to any type but *void*	base type	
address of	&	variable of any type but *void*	pointer to the operand type	
negation	–	arithmetic	arithmetic	
logical not	!	arithmetic or pointer	*int*	
one's complement	~	integral	*int, long,* or *unsigned*	

(continued on the next page)

(Unary operators, continued from the previous page)

Operation	Operator	Operands	Result Type	Notes
increment	++	arithmetic or pointer	arithmetic*	variables of arithmetic types are increased by 1 and those of pointer types by the size (in bytes) of the object they point to; if + + is given before the operand then the operand value is incremented before it is used; otherwise, the value is incremented after it is used
decrement	--	arithmetic or pointer	arithmetic*	same as + + but value is decremented
cast	(*type-name*)	any type	specified type	
size of	sizeof	expression or type name	*unsigned*	use as *sizeof(a)*

Pascal does not have most of the C operators listed above. It has only the dereferencing, negation, and the *logical not* operators.

The *address of* operator is used to extract the address of a variable, i.e., its starting location in memory. This operator is used frequently especially for passing the address of a variable as a function argument to simulate passing arguments "by reference" (i.e., passing "*var* parameters"). We shall discuss this in detail in Chapter 5. Note the following equivalence:

*(&a) ≡ a

where *a* is any variable.

Systems programs often require the ability to manipulate bits of a word. As an example, suppose that a bit in the status word of a device such as printer is to be cleared (set to zero). Unlike Pascal, C provides facilities for bit manipulation. The *one's complement* operator comes in handy for manipulating bits of a word. Consider the following assignment which clears all but the last four bits of the *unsigned* variable *status*:

```
status = status & ~15;
```

The integer constant 15 is stored as the binary constant

```
1111
```

The above assignment could alternatively also have been written using an octal constant as

```
status = status & ~017;
```

We could have also written the above assignment without using the one's complement operator as (assuming that *unsigned* variables are implemented as 16 bit words)

```
status = status & 177760;
```

The *one's complement* operator saves us the trouble of determining the number which has a bit pattern such that all of its bits are ones with the exception of the last four which are zeros. Writing this number explicitly, i.e., without using the one's complement operator, requires knowing the size of a word. Clearing the bits of *status* this way makes the code unportable between machines that have different word sizes.

The C increment and the decrement operators add one to and subtract one from a variable. For example, the expression

```
p++
```

is equivalent to

```
p = p + 1
```

If p is a pointer variable of type T, then adding a one to it implies that p is to be increased by the size of T. Using the cast and the *sizeof* operators, adding one to p is equivalent to the assignment

```
p = (T *) ((int) p + sizeof(T))
```

where $T *$ specifies the type "pointer to T". Notice the ease with which pointers can be converted to integers and integers converted to pointers.

1.4 MULTIPLICATION, DIVISION, ADDITION & SUBTRACTION

Operation	Operator	Operands	Result Type	Notes
multiplication	*	arithmetic	arithmetic*	
division	/	arithmetic	arithmetic*	
remainder	%	integral	integral*	
addition	+	arithmetic types, or pointer and integral types	integral* or pointer	in case of a pointer, the integral operand is multiplied by the size of the pointer's base type before the addition
subtraction	−	arithmetic types, or pointer and integral types, or two identical pointer types	integral* or pointer	in case of a pointer and an integral operand, the integral operand is multiplied by the size of the pointer's base type before subtraction; when one pointer is subtracted from another, the result is divided by the size of the pointer's base type

Unlike Pascal, C does not have a special integer division operator (corresponding to the *div* operator). However, the general C division

---

* The integral or arithmetic type of an operator result conforms to the result type as specified by the "usual arithmetic conversion" rules.

operator can be used for integer division, but if its operands are not integers, then they must be explicitly converted to integers before the division is performed, for instance, as in the expression *"(int) a / (int) b"* where *a* and *b* are floating point expressions.

1.5 SHIFTING BITS

Operation	Operator	Operands	Result Type	Notes
left shift	<<	integral	same as left operand	0-fill for vacated bits
right shift	>>	integral	same as left operand	0-fill for vacated bits if left operand is *unsigned*; otherwise, sign bit is propagated

There are no shift operators in Pascal.

As an illustration of the use of bit shifting, consider the following expression which evaluates to 1 if bit *i* of the variable *status* is on (i.e., it has the value 1); otherwise, it returns 0:

```
status & (i << 1)
```

& is the *bitwise and* operator that "ands" the corresponding pairs of bits of its two operands and for each pair it returns 1 if both the bits are 1; otherwise, it returns 0.

1.6 COMPARISON

Operation	Operator	Operands	Result Type
less than	<	arithmetic or pointer	*int*
greater than	>	arithmetic or pointer	*int*
less than or equal to	<=	arithmetic or pointer	*int*
greater than or equal to	>=	arithmetic or pointer	*int*
equality	==	arithmetic or pointer	*int*
inequality	!=	arithmetic or pointer	*int*

Note that in C "= =" is used as the comparison operator while in Pascal "=" is used.

1.7 BITWISE AND and OR

Operation	Operator	Operands	Result Type
bitwise and	&	integral	integral*
bitwise exclusive or	^	integral	integral*
bitwise inclusive or	|	integral	integral*

There are no bitwise logical operators in Pascal.

The bitwise operators perform logical operations on each of the corresponding pairs of bits of their operands. Note that an *inclusive or* returns 1 if either of the corresponding bits is 1. An *exclusive or* returns 1 only if one of the corresponding bits is 1 but not if both of the bits are 1; otherwise, it returns 0.

1.8 LOGICAL AND and OR

Operation	Operator	Operands	Result Type
logical and	&&	arithmetic or pointer	*int*
logical or	||	arithmetic or pointer	*int*

Unlike the corresponding Pascal logical operators, C logical operators || (or) and && (and) are conditional, that is, their second operands are evaluated only if necessary. For example, if the first operand of the && operator is false, then the second operand will not be evaluated. This is very helpful. As an example, consider the following program fragment that searches an n-element array a for a value x:

```
for (i=0; i<n && a[i] != x; i++)
    ;
```

The following "equivalent" Pascal code will generate a subscript out-of-bounds error because the *and* operator in Pascal always evaluates its second argument:

```
i := 0;
while i < n and a[i] <> x do i:=i+1
```

Evaluating the expression

```
a[i] <> x
```

when i is greater than or equal to n causes the subscript error.

---

*   The integral operator result conforms to the result type as specified by the "usual arithmetic conversion" rules.

1.9 CONDITIONAL EXPRESSION

The conditional expression operator, which has three operands, has the form

$$b \ ? \ e_t \ : \ e_f$$

The result of the above expression is e_t if b is non-zero; otherwise, it is e_f. Expression b must be of an arithmetic type. The other two operands must be of the same type or of types that are automatically convertible to the same type.

The following conditional expression yields the absolute value of variable a:

```
a > 0 ? a : - a
```

There is no equivalent of the conditional expression operator in Pascal. In fact an expression such as the one shown above cannot be written directly. In Pascal, the absolute value of a must be computed and stored in a variable, say *abs*, for later use in an expression:

```
if a > 0
   then abs := a
   else abs := -a;
```

1.10 ASSIGNMENT (SIMPLE & COMPOUND)

Assignment is a statement in Pascal but it is an operator in C.* Unlike Pascal which has only one assignment statement, C has several assignment operators. These operators are classified into two categories: simple and compound. The Pascal assignment statement corresponds to the simple assignment operator; note that Pascal does not have any counterparts of the compound assignment operators.

The simple assignment operator = of C is used as follows:

var = exp

Both variable *var* and expression *exp* must be of arithmetic types, or identical pointer or structure types. In case of arithmetic types, the value of *exp* is converted to the type of *var*. The effect of the above assignment is to assign value *exp* to variable *var*.

The value assigned to the left hand operator is also the result of the above assignment expression. This allows several variables to be assigned the same value using a single C statement as follows:

---

* Note that any C expression can be converted into a statement by appending a semicolon to it.

```
x = y = z = 1.0;
```

In Pascal, the above multiple assignment must be written as three separate assignment statements:

```
x := 1.0;
y := 1.0;
z := 1.0
```

In addition to the simple assignment operator, C has several compound assignment operators. These operators allow assignment expressions of the form

var = var op exp

to be abbreviated as

var op= exp

where *op=* is a compound assignment operator. Here is a list of the C compound assignment operators: $+=$, $-=$, $*=$, $/=$, $\%=$, $>>=$, $<<=$, $\&=$, $^=$, and $|=$.

Compound assignment expressions are not only shorter, but they can be easier to understand and they may help the compiler to generate more efficient code. For example, the C expression

```
x[a>0?a:0] = x[a>0?a:0] + i
```

can be better written as

```
x[a>0?a:0] += i
```

Note the above C assignment would be written in Pascal as

```
if a > 0
    then tmp := a
    else tmp := 0;
x[tmp] := x[tmp] + 1;
```

1.11 COMBINING EXPRESSIONS

Suppose a programmer needs to write multiple expressions in places where the language syntax allows only one expression. For example, only a single expression each is allowed for controlling the *while* loop or the *if* statement. In C, this can be done easily with the comma operator. There is no counterpart of the comma operator in Pascal.

Two expressions e_1 and e_2 can be combined to form a single expression by using the comma operator:

e_1, e_2

The left hand expression e_1 is evaluated first. The type and value of a "comma expression" is the type and value of the right hand expression e_2.

Note that the commas separating variables in definitions and declarations, and separating arguments in function calls are not instances of the comma operator. Comma expressions must be enclosed in parentheses in situations where their use can lead to ambiguous interpretations. For example, when a comma expression is used as a function argument, then it must be enclosed within parentheses.

As an illustration of the comma operator, consider the function *palindrome* given below which determines whether or not a string is palindromic. A palindrome string reads the same whether it is read from left to right or from right to left; for example, strings "mom" and "123454321" are palindromes. Function *palindrome*, which is shown below, returns 1 if its argument *s* is palindromic; otherwise, it returns 0 (stored in file *pal.c*):

```
#include <string.h>
int palindrome(s)
    /*s is the same as reverse(s)*/
    char s[];
{
    int i, j;

    for (i=0, j=strlen(s)-1; i<j; i++, j--)
        if (s[i] != s[j]) return 0;
    return 1;
}
```

The *for* loop statement header takes three arguments: an initial-value expression, a termination condition and a next-value expression. The comma operator is used in the above *for* statement to combine two initial-value expressions and two next-value expressions into single expressions. This example also illustrates the versatility of the C *for* statement when compared to the Pascal *for* statement: with the help of the comma operator, the *for* statement can have two loop variables and two loop increments. This is not possible in Pascal.

For comparison purposes, here is an equivalent Pascal function (stored in *pal.p*):

```
function palindrome(s:alpha; n:integer): boolean;
    var i, j: integer;
        ispal: boolean;
begin
    j := n - 1;
    i := 0;
    ispal := true;
    while ispal and (i<j) do
    begin
        if (s[i] <> s[j])
            then ispal := false;
        i := i + 1;
        j := j - 1
    end;
    palindrome := ispal
end;
```

The above example would have been better written using conformant arrays (as in ISO Pascal) but Turbo Pascal does not support conformant arrays. Note that Turbo Pascal does provide a non-standard facility for allowing arrays of different sizes to be passed as arguments.

In the above function, the string type used is named *alpha* and it is declared as

```
type alpha = packed array[0..10] of char;
```

Note that Turbo Pascal provides a predefined (non-standard) string type named *string* which is a reserved word.

1.12 SYNOPSIS OF OPERATOR PRECEDENCE & ASSOCIATIVITY

The operators are listed in groups of decreasing precedence order:

operators	association
() [] -> .	left to right
! ~ ++ -- (*type*) * & sizeof	right to left
* / %	left to right
+ -	left to right
<< >>	left to right
< <= > >=	left to right
== !=	left to right
&	left to right
^	left to right
|	left to right
&&	left to right
||	left to right
?:	right to left
= += -= *= /= %= >>= <<= &= ^= |=	right to left

Compared to C, Pascal has very few levels of precedence (four to be precise). Moreover, these levels do not conform to normal mathematical conventions as a result of which extra parentheses are often needed when using operators in Pascal. For example, the following C expression

```
i < n && x != 0
```

is written in Pascal as

```
(i < n) and (x <> 0)
```

(We have ignored the difference between the C *&&* and the Pascal *and* operators, i.e., that *&&* is a conditional operator while *and* is an unconditional operator.)

2. EXPRESSIONS

An *expression* is a combination of variables, constants, function calls, operators, and parentheses.

2.1 CONSTANT EXPRESSIONS

Constant expressions are expressions that evaluate to a constant and, moreover, this evaluation can be done at compile time. C requires constant expressions in many places: in array bounds, in initializers, as labels of alternatives in the *switch* statement and in the C preprocessor *#if* statement.

Constant expressions are expressions formed by using only integer, character, and enumeration constants, the *sizeof* operator, the binary operators

+ - * / * & | ^ << >> == != < > <= >=

the unary operators

- ~

and the ternary operator

? :

Parentheses can be used for grouping subexpressions. The unary operator &
can be used in initializers, but the *sizeof* operator cannot be used in
constructing constant expressions for the C preprocessor *#if* statement.

2.2 EXPRESSION EVALUATION

An expression is evaluated in the order specified by the operator precedence
and the associativity (grouping) rules of the programming language. Any
Pascal or C expression may be enclosed within parentheses to override the
precedence and associativity rules. However, in C, parentheses cannot be
used to force the compiler to evaluate expressions in a specific order. As
long as a C compiler obeys the precedence and associativity rules, it is free to
evaluate expressions in any order it likes. If it is important that an expression
be evaluated in a specific order, then the programmer can explicitly specify
this order by using temporary variables and a series of assignment statements
to construct the expression.

3. EXERCISES

1. The following C loop exploits the fact that the *&&* operator evaluates
   its second argument only when *i* is less than *n* to avoid a subscript
   error:

   ```
   for (i=0; i<n && a[i] != x; i++)
       ;
   ```

   How will you write this C loop in Pascal?

2. Write a small program to print the number of bytes used by your C
   compiler to implement *char*, *int*, *long*, *short*, *float*, and *double* types.
   (Hint: use the *sizeof* operator.)

CHAPTER 4

STATEMENTS & INPUT/OUTPUT

Pascal and C have similar statements but there is one important design difference between these two languages. Unlike Pascal, C does not provide input/output statements; instead, input and output is performed by calling functions. These functions are "technically" not part of K&R C but are, instead, part of standard library that comes with every C compiler. (These functions will be included in ANSI C.)

1. STATEMENTS

Pascal statements must be separated by semicolons while every C statement, except executable statements ending with a right curly brace (i.e., compound statements), must be terminated by a semicolon.

1.1 EXPRESSIONS & STATEMENTS

Any C expression can be converted into a statement by appending a semicolon to it. The value of the expression is then simply discarded. C programmers use this "feature" all the time. For instance, procedure calls are constructed from function calls by appending semicolons. The result of a function call, if any (i.e., the function result type is not *void*), is just discarded.

1.2 NULL STATEMENT

In both C and Pascal, a semicolon by itself represents the null statement. The null statement is used in places where the syntax requires the presence of a statement but where a statement is not really necessary.

The null statement is used more in C than in Pascal, especially for specifying null loop bodies. C loops, as we shall see later, are more powerful and more versatile than Pascal loops. Much of the work in a C loop can be accomplished in the loop header itself and a loop body may be unnecessary. As an example, consider the function *strcpy* (stored in file *strcpy.c*), which mimics the functionality of the C library function with the same name:

```
char *strcpy(d, s)
    char d[], s[];
{
    int i;

    for (i=0; i<strlen(s); d[i]=s[i], i++)
        ;
    return d;
}
```

The body of the *for* loop consists of a null statement; all the work is done in the expressions given in the loop header. The loop header consists of three parts: the initial-value expression

```
i=0
```

the loop-termination expression

```
i<strlen(s)
```

and the next-value expression

```
d[i]=s[i], i++
```

The next-value expression consists of two expressions combined with the comma operator. The above *for* statement can alternatively be written without using the comma operator as

```
for (i=0; i<strlen(s); i++)
        d[i] = s[i];
```

which shows the flexibility of C to support a variety of programming paradigms.

Because Pascal does not have the comma operator, it is not possible to write a *for* statement in Pascal that corresponds to the *for* statement used in *strcpy*.

The *null* statement is useful in C because it often allows much work to be done by expressions which in other languages is done using statements.

1.3 ASSIGNMENT STATEMENT

Because C provides the assignment operator, it does not provide a specific statement, as in Pascal, for doing assignment. As mentioned previously, an assignment statement is readily constructed in C by appending a semicolon to an assignment expression, for example,

```
a = 0;
max = a > b ? a : b;
```

When an assignment expression (or any other expression) is converted into a statement by appending a semicolon, the value of the assignment expression is discarded. However, as shown earlier, the fact that assignment is an operator allows multiple assignments to be written as a single statement:

```
a = b = 1;
```

The assignment operator associates from the right, so the effect of the above multiple assignment is to first assign 1 to *b*, and then assign the result of the first assignment (that is, 1) to *a*. Remember that the result of an assignment expression is the value assigned to the variable.

Assignment statements can also be constructed using the compound assignment operators. For example,

```
a[i] += x*y;
i <<= 5;
```

Note that there are many assignment operators in C while there is only assignment statement in Pascal.

1.4 GROUPING STATEMENTS INTO ONE LOGICAL STATEMENT

Curly braces are used in C, instead of the keywords *begin* and *end* as in Pascal, to construct compound statements. Unlike in Pascal, new variables can be defined in C at the beginning of the compound statement. Use of these variables is restricted to the body of the compound statement.

As an example of a compound statement, consider the following code that exchanges the values of two integer variables:

```
  . . .
{
    int tmp;

    tmp = n;
    n = i;
    i = tmp;
}
  . . .
```

The scope of variable *tmp* is restricted to the compound statement. It cannot be accessed outside the compound statement.

1.5 UNRESTRICTED GOTO STATEMENT

Unrestricted *goto* (jump) statements are recognized as being bad for programming because they make programs harder to understand and debug. Consequently, structured programming languages such as Pascal and C provide facilities that decrease the need for using *goto* statements.

Pascal provides only one kind of jump statement: the unrestricted *goto* statement. It does not provide controlled *goto* statements such as a statement to exit from a loop, to continue the next iteration of a loop, or to return from a function from any place within the function. Consequently, in these situations the Pascal programmer has to use *goto* statements or, in an effort to avoid using them, the programmer is forced to use extra variables which may not be very natural.

In addition to the unrestricted *goto* statement, C provides three restricted versions of the *goto* statement: the *break, continue,* and *return* statements. Unrestricted *goto* statements are rarely seen in well-written C programs. Instead, programmers use the restricted versions of the *goto* statement. We shall discuss the *break* and *continue* statements in the next section, and the *return* statement in the next chapter.

Let us now examine the C *goto* statement. Targets of *goto* statements are C executable statements (not definitions and declarations, or C preprocessor statements), which must be explicitly labeled with a prefix of the form

label:

where *label* is an identifier. The use of identifiers, instead of numbers, for labels in C allows programmers to select mnemonic labels. Unlike Pascal labels, C labels do not have to be declared.

The *goto* statement itself has the form

goto *label;*

1.6 RESTRICTED GOTO STATEMENTS: BREAK & CONTINUE

Pascal does not have any restricted *goto* statements while C has three: the *break,* the *continue* and *return* (discussed later) statements. The *break* statement is used in loops and in the *switch* multi-way branch statement. The effect of executing the *break* statement is to exit the immediately surrounding loop or the *switch* statement.

The *continue* statement is used only in loops. It causes the current loop iteration to be abandoned by jumping to the end of the loop body and then begins the next iteration (if allowed by the loop condition).

1.7 IF STATEMENT

The *if* statements in the two languages are similar. As in Pascal, the *else* clause can be omitted. Here is the C *if* statement, with and without the *else* clause:

if (*expression*) *statement*

if (*expression*) *statement* else *statement*

Unless the *if* statement is small, it is not given on a single line. For example, to enhance readability, *if* statements are often written as

```
if  (expression)
      statement
```

```
if  (expression)
      statement
else
      statement
```

Notice that the C *if* statement requires that the *if* expression be enclosed in parentheses and that there is no keyword corresponding to the Pascal keyword *then*.

The C conditional operator is often used instead of the *if* statement for many simple cases. For example, the following *if* statement

```
if (a < b)
    max = b;
else
    max = a;
```

is often written as

```
max = a < b ? b : a;
```

C *if* statements, like Pascal *if* statements, can be nested. As in Pascal, if an *if* statement in C has more *if* clauses than *else* clauses, then any resulting ambiguity is resolved by matching each *else* clause with the closest and innermost *if* clause that has not been matched as yet.

As an example of nested *if* statements in C, consider the following function *grade* that takes a numeric grade (between 0 and 100) and converts it to a letter grade (stored in file *grade.c*):

```c
char grade(i)
      int i;
{
    if (i > 100 || i < 0) {
        printf("grade:error, bad score=%d\n",i);
        exit(1);
    }
    else if (i > 85)
        return 'A';
    else if (i > 70)
        return 'B';
    else if (i > 55)
        return 'C';
    else if (i > 40)
        return 'D';
    else
        return 'F';
}
```

Curly braces are used in the true alternative of the *if* statement shown above to combine two statements into one logical statement. Remember that the C syntax allows only a single statement each for the *if* alternatives. The *exit* function call terminates the program.

Notice that judicious use of indentation improves program readability. The indentation style used here for the nested *if* statements is not the same as shown earlier; there is no need to be rigid. You may use any reasonable indentation style, but whatever style you use, be consistent.

1.8 SWITCH STATEMENT

The C *switch* statement is a multi-way branch statement which is the counterpart of the Pascal *case* statement. The C *switch* statement has the form

```
switch (exp) {
case-label₁: statements₁
case-label₂: statements₂
    ...
case-labelₙ: statementsₙ
}
```

where *exp* is an integer expression and each *case-label$_i$* has either the form

```
case const
```

where *const* is an integral constant or consists of just the keyword

```
default
```

Duplicate labels are not allowed in the *switch* statement. Execution of a *switch* statement proceeds as follows: evaluate the *switch* expression *exp* and jump to a *case* label that has an integer constant equal to *exp* and start executing the statements from that point onwards. If there is no such label, then jump to the *default* label and start executing statements from that point onwards. If there is no matching *case* label and there is no *default* label, then the *switch* statement behaves like the null statement.

Although the Pascal *case* statement and the C *switch* statement provide similar functionality, they differ in important ways:

1. In the *switch* statement, control flows on from one alternative to the next. The *break* statement is normally used to terminate execution of (i.e., exit from) the *switch* statement after an alternative has completed execution. (Note that the *continue* and *return* statements can also be used instead of the *break* statement.) Execution of the Pascal *case* statement automatically terminates after the execution of an alternative. There is no need for an explicit jump statement after each alternative.

2. Standard Pascal does not provide for the specification of a default alternative, i.e., an alternative that should be executed in the event no label matches the *case* expression. C provides a *default* alternative as do some Pascal implementations, e.g., Turbo Pascal.

3. Unlike in Pascal, *switch* alternative labels cannot be subranges. Each label must be listed explicitly.

As an example of the C *switch* statement consider the following code that prints asterisks [Harb84]:

```
switch (x) {
    case 1: printf("*\n");
    case 2: printf("**\n");
    case 3: printf("***\n");
    case 4: printf("****\n");
}
```

If *x* has the value 1, then 10 asterisks will be printed, if it has the value 2 then 9 asterisks will be printed, and so on. This is because execution of an alternative (one of the *printf* statements) does not complete execution of the *switch* statement; instead, the remaining alternatives are then executed. To leave the *switch* statement right after executing an alternative, a *break* statement must be given explicitly as the last statement in the alternative:

```
switch (x) {
    case 1: printf("*\n");
            break;
    case 2: printf("**\n");
            break;
    case 3: printf("***\n");
            break;
    case 4: printf("****\n");
            break;
}
```

Now, if *x* has the value *i* (between 1 and 4), then only *i* asterisks will be printed.

To execute only the statements associated with a *case* label, the following form of the *switch* statement should be used:

```
switch (exp) {
    case const:  statements
                 break;
    case const:  statements
                 break;
...
    case const:  statements
                 break;
    default:     statements
}
```

There is no need to give a *break* statement after the *default* alternative because, as shown above, it is given as the last alternative. Instead of using the *break* statement to exit from a *switch* statement alternative, you can, if appropriate, also exit by using the *continue* or *return* statements. The effect of exiting with the *continue* statement is to go on to the next iteration of the immediately enclosing loop and the effect of exiting with the *return* statement is to return from the function containing the *switch* statement.

A *switch* statement can have multiple *case* labels for the same alternative, but there must be no duplicate *case* labels.

As another example of the *switch* statement, consider the following program (stored in file *wc.c*) which counts the total number of characters, words, lines, spaces, tabs, and punctuation characters in the input:

```
#include <stdio.h>
#include <string.h>
main()
{
    int c, n = 0, nsp = 0, nwd = 0,
        nl = 0, nt = 0, np = 0;
    while ((c = getchar()) != EOF) {
        n++;
        switch (c) {
        case ' ':
            nsp++; nwd++; break;
        case '\n':
            nl++; nwd++; break;
        case '\t':
            nt++; nwd++; break;
        default:
            if (ispunct(c)) np++;
        }
    }
    printf("chars=%d, words=%d, lines=%d\n",
                            n, nwd, nl);
    printf("spaces=%d, tabs=%d, punct=%d\n",
                            nsp, nt, np);
}
```

The above program is straightforward and it uses a simple algorithm that does not cover all possible situations. For example, every time a space is encountered, the word count is increased by one. This strategy for counting words is fine if all the words are separated by a single space, but if there are multiple spaces between words, then the word count will be incorrect. (How will you refine the above algorithm to take care of multiple spaces between words?)

Notice that the function *ispunct* is used in the *switch* statement to avoid listing the *case* labels explicitly for each one of the punctuation characters. The reason for this is simple: listing the case labels explicitly for each of the punctuation marks will be long and tedious.

1.9 LOOP STATEMENTS: WHILE, FOR, & DO

Both Pascal and C have three kinds of loops: the *while* loop, the *for* loop and the *do-while* (called *repeat-until* in Pascal) loop. The C *for* loop is much more powerful than the Pascal *for* loop but the other two loops are similar.

1.9.1 THE WHILE LOOP. Let us start by first discussing the *while* loop. Except for the slight difference in the syntax, the *while* loops in C and Pascal are quite similar. The C *while* loop has the form

```
while (expression) statement
```

Unlike the Pascal *while* loop, the C *while* loop requires parentheses around its expression.

As an example of a *while* loop, consider the following C code that sets variable *i* to the index of the array element whose value is equal to that of *key*; otherwise, if there is no such element, the value of *i* is set to *MAX* which is the size of the array:

```
while (i < MAX && a[i] != key)
    i++;
```

Notice the use of the conditional *and* operator && to ensure that array *a* is referenced only if *i* is less than *MAX*.

1.9.2 THE FOR LOOP. The C *for* loop has the form

```
for (initial-value; termination; next-value)
    statement
```

The three expressions *initial-value, termination,* and *next-value* control execution of the *for* loop as explained below:

1. Expression *initial-value* is evaluated once at the beginning of the loop. Typically this expression is used to assign initial values to the loop variables.

2. Expression *termination* is evaluated. If this expression is true (non-zero), then the loop body is executed; otherwise, the *for* loop is terminated.

3. After the loop body has been executed, expression *next-value* is evaluated. Typically this expression is used to update values of the loop variables. Execution of the loop continues with step 2.

As an example of the C *for* loop, consider the following function *sum* that computes the sum of a 2-dimensional array:

```
int sum(a, m, n)
    int a[][N], m, n;
{
    int i, j, total = 0;

    for (i=0; i<m; i++)
        for (j=0; j<n; j++)
            total += a[i][j];
    return total;
}
```

The two nested *for* loops generate a pair of indices, one for each element of the array *a*. The body of each *for* loop consists of one statement. The body of the first *for* loop is the second *for* loop. Notice that 2-dimensional arrays can be passed as arguments to functions and that only the size of the first dimension of the array can be left unspecified.

In C the *for* loop is really another way of writing the *while* loop. This leads to a subtle semantic difference between the Pascal and C *for* loops. Consider the following Pascal *for* loop:

```
for i := 0 to N do ...
```

Expression N, which represents the termination value of the loop variable i, is evaluated only once: upon entry to the *for* statement. Changing the value of N in the body of the loop has no effect on the number of iterations that will be performed. Now consider the C equivalent of the above loop:

```
for (i=0; i<N; i++) ...
```

The termination expression $i<N$ is evaluated at the beginning of each iteration. Changing the value of N in the body of the loop changes the number of iterations that will be performed.

Any or all of the three *for* loop expressions can be omitted. A true value is assumed for any omitted expression. One or more of these expressions are often omitted. For example, it is common to see a loop of the form

```
for (;;) {
  ...
}
```

This loop, a "forever" or a non-terminating loop, will not terminate by itself; it must be terminated explicitly by exiting from the loop (for example, by using a *break* statement or a *return* statement).

Often a C preprocessor *#define* statement is used to make the forever nature of the loop shown above more explicit:

```
#define forever for(;;)
  ...
forever { /*forever is replaced by for(;;)*/
  ...
}
```

Of course, as is done in Pascal, you can also write a non-terminating loop using the C *while* loop:

```
while (1) {
  ...
}
```

The C *for* loop is more flexible and more versatile than the Pascal *for* loop because the *for* loop expressions can be arbitrary expressions that can be omitted or that can consist of multiple expressions combined with the comma operator. For example, the *next-value* expression is not restricted to changing the value of the loop variable by one: the value of the C *for* loop variable can be changed as desired.

To illustrate the power of the C *for* loop, we will write a program fragment to compute the square root of a floating point number a using the following algorithm (due to Newton):

1. Let *new* represent the current approximation of a's square root; as a first approximation of the a's square root, set *new* to $0.5*a$.

2. Improve the square root approximation by setting *old* to *new* and setting *new* to $0.5*(old+a/old)$.

3. Repeat step 2 as long as necessary. Typically, a stopping point used for this iteration is when the difference between *old* and *new* becomes very small, say 0.001.

Here is a program fragment, based on the above algorithm, that computes the square root:

```
for (new=a/2, old=0.0; abs(old-new)>0.001;) {
   old = new;
   new = 0.5*(old+a/old);
}
```

Notice the absence of the *next-value* expression (the third expression) in the *for* statement. The loop variables are assigned their next values in the loop body. Alternatively, these assignments could have been made into a *next-value* expression and the loop could have been given a null body:

```
for (new=a/2, old=0.0; abs(old-new)>0.001;
                  old=new, new=0.5*(old+a/old))
   ;
```

The comma operator guarantees that its left operand will be evaluated first.

1.9.3 THE DO-WHILE LOOP. The third C loop, the *do-while* loop, which is the counterpart of the Pascal *repeat-until* loop, has the form

do *statement* while (*expression*);

The *do-while* loop executes its *body* until the specified expression becomes false. This expression is evaluated after each execution of the loop body. Consequently, the loop body is always executed at least once. This is the main difference between the *do-while* loop, and the *for* and *while* loops. As in the case of the other two C loops, a compound statement can be used when the loop body consists of more than one statement.

Here is an example of the *do-while* loop in which function *send* is called at least once:

```
do send(c = getchar()); while (c != EOF);
```

2. INPUT/OUTPUT

Input and output is done in C by calling standard library functions that come with every C compiler. C input/output facilities are more extensive than those in Pascal. For example, unlike Pascal, C provides a facility for formatted input and its formatted output facility is more elaborate than that of Pascal. Also, unlike Pascal, C provides facilities for reading and writing random-access files.

2.1 END OF LINE & END OF FILE

An important difference between doing input and output in Pascal and C is the treatment of "end of line" and "end of file". In Pascal, the end of a line is sensed with the *eoln* function, the *readln* statement can be used to skip to the next input line, the *writeln* statement can be used to write output on a new line or move to a new line, and the end of a file is sensed with the *eof* function.

C adopts a different approach which is quite elegant. It introduces the notion of the newline character, denoted as "\n", which is the combination of the carriage return and line feed characters. The end of an input line can be determined in a C program by testing the last character read for the newline character. Skipping to a new line just means reading past the newline character. Moving to a new output line is accomplished by simply writing the newline character.

As an example illustrating uses of the newline character, consider the following program which counts the number of lines in the input file (stored in *lines.c*):

```c
#include <stdio.h>
main()
{
    int c, n = 0;

    while ((c = getchar()) != EOF)
        if (c == '\n') n++;
    printf("number of lines = %d\n", n);
}
```

Notice that the newline character is treated just like the other characters.

The above program uses a constant *EOF* (mnemonic for end of file) which is defined in the file *stdio.h* to have the value –1. Function *getchar* returns –1 when it encounters the end of file. This is the paradigm used by C functions to indicate an end of file. The C paradigm for indicating an end of file is quite different from that of Pascal in which the function *eof* must be called to determine if the end of file has been encountered.

2.2 INPUT/OUTPUT FACILITIES

Both Pascal and C provide a wide variety of facilities for reading from and writing to files, reading from the keyboard and writing to the display. As mentioned earlier, input/output facilities are provided in C as library functions which come with every C compiler.

Like Pascal, C does not provide facilities for directly interacting with the computer hardware. However, these facilities can be written easily in C. Also many C compilers, like Pascal compilers, often provide non-standard functions for interacting with the computer hardware. For example, the Lattice C compiler provides a set of non-standard functions called the console I/O functions [Latt83].

Pascal provides facilities only for accessing sequential files. C, on the other hand, provides elaborate facilities for accessing both sequential and random access files. Pascal provides special versions of the input/output statements for dealing with new lines in text files and skipping to a new page. There is no need for special versions of input/output functions in C because, unlike in Pascal, the newline and formfeed ("newpage") characters are read and written just like the other characters.

Three files are automatically made available to every C program. These are the standard input, standard output, and standard error files. All other files must be explicitly opened and closed. However, unlike in Pascal, there is no need to give the names of external files that will be accessed in the program as program arguments. External file names in C are just strings: these names can be passed as command-line arguments, read in as input, or even generated internally.

The standard input file is associated, by default, with the keyboard, and can be explicitly referenced by the name *stdin*. This identifier is declared in the standard input header file *stdio.h*. Similarly, the standard output and error files are both associated with the display. They can be explicitly referenced using the names *stdout* and *stderr* which are also declared in *stdio.h*. (Note that *stdin*, *stdout*, and *stderr* are actually constants of type *FILE* ∗.) Normal output is written to *stdout*. Error messages are written to *stderr* so they can be separated from the normal output by redirecting *stdout* or *stderr* (note that the MS-DOS system does not support the redirection of *stderr*).

Many C programs are written so that they read input from *stdin* and write output to *stdout*. Standard input/output redirection can then be used to read input from a file instead of from the keyboard and write output to a file instead of to the display.

As an example of input/output and its redirection, consider the following program (stored in file *roots.c*) for computing the roots of a quadratic equation:

```
#include <stdio.h>
#include <math.h>

char f1[]="error, %g, %g, %g have complex roots\n";
char f2[]="coeff = %g, %g, %g, roots = %g, %g\n";
main()
{
    double a, b, c, r1, r2, tmp;
    int n;

    while ((n=scanf("%lf%lf%lf", &a, &b, &c))==3){
        if ((tmp = b*b - 4*a*c) < 0) {
            fprintf(stderr, f1, a, b, c);
            continue;
        }
        else
            tmp = sqrt(tmp);
        r1 = (-b+tmp)/(2*a);
        r2 = (-b-tmp)/(2*a);
        printf(f2, a, b, c, r1, r2);
    }
    if (n != EOF) {
        fprintf(stderr,"error, missing coeff\n");
        exit(1);
    }
    exit(0);
}
```

Function *fprintf* is used to print error messages on the standard error file, that is, on the display. Error messages are not printed on the standard output file (say by using the *printf* function) because this would force error messages to be redirected to a file along with the rest of the output. This may delay discovery of the error in the input data. Also, characters written to *stderr* are usually not buffered as are characters written to *stdout*; they are printed immediately. (Buffering is used to speed up program execution by reducing the number of interactions with other system components, e.g., disks and displays.)

Note that the function call

```
printf(fmt2, a, b, c, r1, r2);
```

is equivalent to the function call

```
fprintf(stdout, fmt2, a, b, c, r1, r2);
```

Some other items of interest are the use of the arrays *fmt1* and *fmt2* to store the formats that are used by the *fprintf* and *printf* function calls to print error messages, and the coefficients and the roots (note that preprocessor constant definitions could also have been used for the format strings). Function *exit* is called to terminate the program explicitly. If function *exit* is not called explicitly, then it will be called automatically, but its exit status (the argument supplied to *exit*) will be garbage. The exit value can be used at the MS-DOS command level to determine whether or not the program executed successfully. In case of the Lattice C compiler, the exit value shows up as the value of the MS-DOS variable *errorlevel* [Latt86].

Here is some sample input (stored in file *roots.dat*) that will be used for program *roots*:

```
1 -4 4
1 0 1
2 5 -2
2 1 7
6 3
```

Executing *roots* with this data by using the command

```
roots <roots.dat
```

produces the following output on the terminal:

```
coeff = 1, -4, 4, roots = 2, 2
error, 1, 0, 1 have complex roots
coeff = 2, 5, -2, roots = 0.350781, -2.850781
error, 2, 1, 7 have complex roots
error, missing coeff
```

In this case, the error messages are printed on the display even if the standard output is redirected as shown below:

```
roots <roots.dat >roots.res
```

The output produced on the display is

```
error, 1, 0, 1 have complex roots
error, 2, 1, 7 have complex roots
error, missing coeff
```

and the output written to file *roots.res* is

```
coeff = 1, -4, 4, roots = 2, 2
coeff = 2, 5, -2, roots = 0.350781, -2.850781
```

On the MS-DOS system, *stderr* cannot be redirected; output written to the standard error file will always be displayed on the screen. On some systems standard error output can be redirected to a file just like standard output can be redirected to a file.

To read from and write to files other than the standard input (*stdin*), standard output (*stdout*), and standard error (*stderr*) files, the following steps must be followed:

   1. Include the header file *stdio.h* (using the *#include* instruction).

2. Declare a *FILE* * type variable for each file.

3. Open the file for reading or writing, as appropriate, using the file open function *fopen*: this function takes as arguments the file name and a string indicating how the file is to be accessed. It returns a value that identifies the opened file. Save this value in the file variable and use this variable to access the file.

4. The file can be accessed as a stream of characters (with functions such as *fgetc*, *fscanf*, *fputc*, and *fprintf*) or as a random access file for reading and writing blocks of data at appropriate places within the file (using functions such as *fseek*, *rewind*, *fread*, and *fwrite*).

5. Finally, after file accesses have been completed, the file should be closed (using function *fclose*). If the file is not closed explicitly, then it will be closed automatically upon program termination. But remember that only a small number of files (about 15) can be open at any given time. If a large number of files are being manipulated in the program, then it is a good idea to close files that are not needed any more.

2.3 COMMONLY USED C INPUT/OUTPUT FUNCTIONS

A partial list of the C file access functions is given below. For a complete list and a detailed explanation of each function see Appendix 1. These file access functions can be classified into three categories: input, output, and file manipulation and file status query.

First, here are the input functions:

fgets	Get a string from a file.
fread	Read blocks from a file.
getc	Get a character from a file.
getchar	Get a character from *stdin*.
gets	Get a string from *stdin*.
fscanf	Read formatted input from a file.
scanf	Read formatted input from *stdin*.
sprintf	Write formatted output to a string.

Now, here are the output functions:

fprintf	Write formatted output to a file.
fputc	Write a character to a file.
fputs	Write a string to a file.

fwrite   Write blocks to a file.

printf   Write formatted output to *stdout*.

putc   Write a character to a file.

putchar Write a character to *stdout*.

puts   Write a string to *stdout*.

sscanf Read formatted input from a string.

Finally, here are the file manipulation and file status query functions:

fclose Close a file.

feof   End-of-file check.

ferror Error check.

fflush Flush output buffer.

fopen   Open a file.

See Appendix 1 for a comprehensive list and a detailed explanation of the input/output functions provided in the standard C library.

3. EXERCISES

1. Write a function *max* that computes the maximum element of a floating point array. Test it by writing a *main* function that defines and initializes an array, then calls *max* with the array as an argument, and then prints the maximum value in the array.

2. Give reasons to support the claim that the C *for* statement is more powerful and flexible than the Pascal *for* statement.

3. What are the advantages and disadvantages of the C *switch* statement compared to the Pascal *case* statement.

CHAPTER 5

FUNCTIONS & FILES

Pascal has both functions and procedures, but C has only functions. Notably, the lack of procedures in C is not really a problem since C functions that do not return a value (to be precise, functions that return the *void* type) are just like procedures. Actually, any C function can be treated like a procedure because if its return value is not used then this value is simply discarded.

Functions and files are the modularization facilities provided in C for partitioning programs into smaller components. Functions allow the executable part of a program to be partitioned into smaller components. And files are modules that can be used to group together logically related functions, definitions, and declarations. Files are also the compilation units, i.e., program components that can be independently compiled.

The C counterpart of the Pascal main *program* is the function with the distinguished name *main*. Unlike standard Pascal programs, C programs can be passed arguments when they are invoked; i.e., C supports command-line arguments.

C terminology for referring to function parameters is different from the terminology used in Pascal. Actual parameters are called arguments and formal parameters are called parameters. An important difference between C and Pascal is that C does not have the notion of *var* parameters. However, *var* parameters can easily be simulated in C by passing addresses of variables and using pointers.

Unlike Pascal functions, C functions cannot be nested. The Pascal approach gives the programmer more control on function visibility by allowing functions to be nested within functions that use them. However, in practice the lack of function nesting does not seem to be much of a disadvantage.

1. C FUNCTION FACILITIES

C provides two sets of facilities for writing functions: pure functions and macros. The macro facility is provided by the C preprocessor. Macros are like functions except that macro calls are replaced textually, before the compilation phase, by their bodies after appropriately substituting arguments for parameters. Macros are essentially in-line functions. Macros are faster than functions, because they avoid the need for instructions for jumping to and returning from the macro body. There is a price that may have to be paid for this speedup, however: the macro bodies replacing the calls can take up more storage. Macros will be discussed in detail in Chapter 7.

2. FUNCTION DEFINITIONS

We have already seen several examples of C function definitions. Now here is the general form of C function definitions:

result-type   function-name (*parameters*)
        parameter declarations
{
        type declarations, variable definitions, & declarations
        statements
}

The first line of the function definition can be prefixed by the keyword *static* to restrict the scope of the function to the file containing it.

A function can have zero or more parameters. The part of the function enclosed within curly braces is called the *function body*. Variables defined inside a function body are called local variables, and their scope is limited to the function body. Like the scope of local variables, the scope of function parameters is limited to the function body. In fact, function parameters are very much like local variables. Variables declared or defined outside a function body but in the same file as the function are called global variables and can be referenced from within the function. The scope of an *external* global variable spans across multiple files while that of a *static* global variable is restricted to the file containing the variable definition. The scope of types declared within a function body is restricted to the function body; the scope of types declared outside the function body is restricted to the file containing the function body.

2.1 MAIN FUNCTION & COMMAND-LINE ARGUMENTS

Each C program must have a function named *main* (corresponding to the Pascal *program* statement). This is the function that is first called when a program starts executing. Unlike in standard Pascal, arguments can be passed from the operating system (such as MS-DOS) command line to the C program, i.e., to function *main*. The operating system calls *main* with two arguments: *argc*, which is the number of command-line arguments, and *argv*, which is an array of pointers to strings, each of which points to one command-line argument. The command name is always passed as the first argument, in string *argv[0]*. Consequently, the value of *argc* is always at least one.

As an example of a program that is called with command-line arguments, consider the following program that counts and prints the number of characters and lines in each file (stored in file *fcnt.c*):

```
/*count number of characters & lines in files*/
#include <stdio.h>
main(argc, argv)
    int argc;
    char *argv[];
{
    int i, nc, nl, c;
            /*nc = no of char, nl = no oflines*/
    FILE *fp;

    nc = nl = 0;
    for (i=1; i < argc; i++)
    {
        if ((fp=fopen(argv[i], "r")) == NULL) {
            printf("Invalid file %s\n",argv[i]);
            continue;
        }
        while ((c=getc(fp)) != EOF){
            if (c == '\n')
                nl++;
            nc++;
        }
        printf("%s: chars=%d, lines=%d\n",
                            argv[i], nc, nl);

        fclose(fp);
    }
}
```

After the character and line counting program is compiled and linked to produce an executable file *fcnt*, it is invoked as

fcnt *file₁* *file₂* ... *fileₙ*

For example, the command

fcnt fcnt.c

counts the number of characters and lines in file *fcnt.c* which contains the C program shown above.

3. FUNCTION DECLARATIONS

In C, as in Pascal, either the definition of a function or its declaration must appear in the program before the function can be referenced. A function declaration is given if the function definition is contained in another file, or if the definition appears after a function reference. Function declarations play a role similar to that played by the Pascal *forward* directive.

Function declarations are of the form

result-type   function-name **( ) ;**

For C library functions, header files containing function declarations are normally provided, and these files should be included instead of giving explicit function declarations in files that contain references to these functions.

A function declaration helps the compiler generate correct code for the function result and allows it to check whether or not the function result is being used correctly with respect to its type. However, in K&R C, neither the function parameters nor their types are given in the function declaration. Consequently, it is not possible for the C compiler to check whether or not a function is called with the right number of parameters nor can it check if the argument types are correct. Recognizing this deficiency, ANSI C will require the parameter types to be listed in the function declaration.

4. FUNCTION CALLS

C function calls, like Pascal function calls, have the form

function-name (*arguments*)

Functions calls can be used in expressions (assuming they return a value of a type other than *void*) or they can be converted to statements by appending a semicolon. In the latter case, the function result is simply discarded.

5. ARGUMENT PASSING

All function arguments are passed by value in C. This means that each argument is evaluated and its result copied to the corresponding parameter. Any changes to the parameter itself have no effect on the corresponding argument. C does not support passing arguments by reference, i.e., there are no *var* parameters in C.

Pointers and variable addresses are used to simulate *var* parameters in C. Changing the object pointed to by a pointer parameter changes the object pointed to by the corresponding pointer argument. This is because both the parameter and the argument have the same pointer value, i.e., they point to the same object. Consequently, to change the value of a variable by calling a function, the address of the variable must be passed to the function.

In case of an array argument, the array is not copied. Instead, a pointer to the beginning of the array is copied to the parameter. This is because an array name is actually a pointer to the beginning of the array. Thus, from a practical viewpoint, one can assume that arrays are passed by reference in C.

To illustrate the argument passing mechanism of C, we shall write a function *cube* that cubes its argument. First, here is the Pascal version of *cube* (stored in file *cube.p*):

```
procedure cube(var x: real);
begin
    x := x*x*x
end
```

Now let us suppose that we write the function *cube* in C as (stored in file *cube0.c*):

```
void cube(x)
    double x;
{
    x = x*x*x;
}
```

cube, as written above, will not work correctly because *x* is passed by value. Consider a call to *cube*:

```
cube(a);
```

Argument *a* is copied into the parameter *x* which is then cubed. However, argument *a* is not cubed; in fact, nothing happens to *a*. We have two choices in modifying *cube* so that it does actually give us the cube of the argument supplied:

- *cube* can return as its result the cube of its argument which can then be assigned to the variable passed as the argument.

- *cube* can be given the address of the variable to be cubed; *cube* can use this address to cube the variable.

Here is the first solution (stored in file *cube1.c*):

```
double cube(x)
    double x;
{
    return x*x*x;
}
```

Here is how a variable will be cubed:

```
a = cube(a);
```

Now here is the second solution (stored in file *cube2.c*):

```
void cube(x)
    double *x;
{
    (*x) = (*x)*(*x)*(*x);
}
```

The address of the variable to be cubed is passed to *cube*:

```
cube(&a);
```

In the function body, parameter *x* refers to the address of *a* and *x is therefore an alias for *a*. This is how *var* parameters are simulated in C. The programmer gives the address of the variable, instead of the variable itself, in a function call. In Pascal, the programmer gives a variable in a subprogram call to match a *var* parameter; the compiler then passes the address (not the value) of this variable to the subprogram. In C the address of the argument is passed to the function. In the function body, the programmer must explicitly dereference the parameter representing the variable address to access the variable. In Pascal, the programmer does not have to do the dereferencing for a *var* parameter, because it is done by the compiler.

Let us now consider how to change the value of a pointer variable by calling a function. As discussed above, the address of the pointer variable (a pointer to the pointer), and not the pointer variable itself, must be given as an argument to the function in question. Suppose that we want to write a function *alloc* that encapsulates the following code:

```
char *p;
int n;
   ...
if ((p = malloc(n)) != NULL) {
    puts("not enough heap storage\n");
    exit(1);
}
```

Here is one possible definition for function *alloc*:

```
void alloc(pp, n)
    char **pp;
    int n;
{
    if ((*pp = malloc(n)) != NULL) {
        puts("not enough heap storage\n");
        exit(1);
    }
}
```

Notice that the first parameter is a pointer to a character pointer and not just a character pointer. To set character pointer *p* to point to *n* bytes of allocated storage, *alloc* must be called with the address of *p*:

```
alloc(&p, n);
```

6. FUNCTION RESULT & COMPLETION

In Pascal, the value returned by a function, that is, the function result, is the value assigned to the function name. C adopts a different approach: the function result is the value specified with the *return* statement which has the form

```
return e;
```

The type of expression *e* must match the function type (or it should be convertible to the function type according to the "usual arithmetic conversion" rules).

Functions with a *void* result type (these functions are the counterparts of the Pascal procedures) can complete execution either by completing execution of the program body or by executing a *return* statement of the form

```
return;
```

C functions that return a result (i.e., the result type is not *void*) must complete execution by executing the *return* statement. Such functions must not terminate by just completing execution of the function body; otherwise, the value returned by the function will be garbage.

A function can have several *return* statements.

7. RECURSION

Like Pascal, C supports recursion; that is, C allows a function to call itself. The basic idea behind recursion is to decompose a problem into smaller subproblems which are then solved by recursively calling the function that was called to solve the original problem. Recursion is an important programming tool because many algorithms are naturally recursive.

To illustrate recursion, we will implement a recursive version of the binary search example given in Chapter 2 (stored in file *rsearch.c*):

```
/*search sorted array a for value x; return*/
/*k such that a[k]==x; otherwise, return -1*/

int search(a, l, u, x)
    int a[], l, u, x;
{
    int k;

    if (l > u)
        return -1;
    else if (a[k = (l+u)/2] == x)
        return k;
    else if (a[k] < x)
        search(a, k+1, u, x);
    else
        search(a, l, k-1, x);
}
```

Function *search* searches an ordered array *a* for an element with a value equal to *x*. *a* is assumed to be sorted in increasing order. *search* starts off by checking to see whether or not the middle element of a is equal to x. If it is, then the search is complete. Otherwise, depending upon whether the middle element of a is less than or greater than x, function *search* is called recursively to search either the upper or lower half of a.

Recursive calls should be made conditionally, that is, only when some conditions are satisfied. If a recursive call is made unconditionally, that is, a function calls itself every time it is called, then the recursion will never end (the function will call itself again and again forever). Of course, a program containing such a function will eventually terminate (in an error state) by running out of storage. Note that a certain amount of storage has to be allocated for every function call. Amongst other things, this storage is used for the function arguments, for the automatic variables in the function, and for saving the address of the instruction to be executed after the function has completed execution.

8. STATIC VARIABLES

Local variables are, by default, automatic variables. They are automatically allocated afresh every time a function is called and deallocated when the function completes execution. Consequently, automatic variables do not retain values across function calls.

All Pascal variables are automatic variables. However, C local variables that are qualified with the storage class *static*, i.e., function static variables, retain their values across function calls. Global variables can also be used to do the same thing but, unlike local static variables, their scope is not restricted to a single function.

As an example illustrating the use of a local static variable, consider a multi-user operating system such as the UNIX system in which many users simultaneously share the same computer. The operating system executes each user's command for a fraction of a second (or some other time unit) before going on to the next user. This fraction is called a *time slice* and this strategy of sharing a computer between several users is called *time sharing*. If the computer is powerful enough, then time sharing will give each user the illusion that the user has a dedicated (single-user) computer. One way of picking the next user to get a time slice is to search an array called the *process table* (*user table*) which contains information about all user programs. To make sure that each user gets a time slice in turn, the process table is searched sequentially for the next user starting just after the position, in the process table, of the last user to get a time slice. A local static variable, say *lastuser*, is used to remember the index of the last user. The search for the next user is started with the index value *lastuser*+1. Here is a function for picking the next user (stored in file *nextuser.c*):

```
extern int user[]; /*user table*/
extern int n;      /*table size*/

int nextuser()
{
    static lastuser = 0;

    while (1)
    {
        lastuser = ++lastuser % n;
        if (user[lastuser] != (-1))
          /*user[i] == -1 indicates empty slot*/
            return lastuser;
    }
}
```

Local static variables should be initialized in their definitions (the compiler will initialize them at compile time). Initialization with assignment statements is ineffective because, each time a function is called, these statements will be re-executed thus destroying the previous values of the local static variables.

Note that the integer array *user* and the integer variable *n* are external variables which must be defined in another file that will be compiled independently and linked with the compiled version of the file *nextuser.c*.

9. COMMUNICATION BETWEEN FUNCTIONS

In addition to communicating by means of parameters, functions can also communicate by using global variables. As mentioned earlier, there are two kinds of global variables in C: *file static* and *external* variables. File static variables are used for communicating between functions in the same file. The scope of file static global variables is restricted to the file containing them. External variables can be used to communicate between any two functions in a program even though they may be in different files.

To illustrate the use of a file static variable, we will give the skeleton code for implementing a pseudo-random number generator. The random number generator consists of two functions: *newseed* which is called to set the random number seed, that is, the initial value used for generating the random number sequence, and *random* which returns the next random number (between 0 and 9 in our example). Here are the two random generator functions which are stored in the same file:

```
static int seed = 0;

void newseed(i)
    int i;
{
    seed = i;
}

int random()
{
    seed = compute random number using seed;
    return seed % 10;
            /*random number between 0 & 9*/
}
```

We have not shown you the code for generating the random number. Generating "good" random number sequences is not easy. The reader interested in learning more about random numbers is referred to the classic *The Art of Computer Programming* (Volume 2) by D. E. Knuth [Knut69].

External variables are used primarily for communication between functions stored in different files. For each external variable, one file must contain its definition and each of the other files must contain a matching declaration. By default, a variable definition given outside a function is an external definition. The presence of the keyword *extern* distinguishes an external declaration from an external definition.

Suppose that the above random number generation functions are stored in separate files. If variable *seed* is to be accessible to both functions, it will have to be defined as an external variable. Here is the file containing the definition of the external variable *seed* and the definition of function *newseed*:

```
int seed = 0;

void newseed(i)
    int i;
{
    seed = i;
}
```

An initial value for an external variable can be given in its definition but not in its declaration.

Here is the file containing a matching declaration of the external variable *seed* and the definition of function *random*:

```
extern int seed;

int random()
{
    seed =    compute random number using seed;
    return seed % 10;
                /*random number between 0 & 9*/
}
```

10. FUNCTION NAMES AS ARGUMENTS

As in Pascal, a function can be passed in C as an argument to other functions by just giving the function name as an argument. A function name is really a pointer to the code for executing the function. As an example, suppose we want to write a function *printrange* (stored in file *printrng.c*) that prints the values of a function argument between the specified limits *a* and *b* using an interval equal to *step*:

```
#include <stdio.h>
void printrange(pf, a, b, step, fname)
    double (*pf)(), a, b, step;
    char *fname;
{
    double x;

    for (x = a; x <= b; x += step)
        printf("%s(%g) = %g\n",fname,x,(*pf)(x));
}
```

Here is an example use of this function:

```
double dbl(x)   /*returns 2*x*/
    double x;
{
    return 2*x;
}

main()
{
    double a = 1, b = 10, step = 1;
    printrange(dbl, a, b, step, "dbl");
}
```

Because function *dbl* was defined before it was used, it was not necessary to declare it. Had its definition been given after that of function *main*, then it would have been necessary to declare it:

```
main()
{
    double dbl(), a = 1, b = 10, step = 1;
    printrange(dbl, a, b, step, "dbl");
}

double dbl(x)   /* returns 2*x */
    double x;
{
    return 2*x;
}
```

Here is the output of the above program:

```
dbl(1)  = 2
dbl(2)  = 4
dbl(3)  = 6
dbl(4)  = 8
dbl(5)  = 10
dbl(6)  = 12
dbl(7)  = 14
dbl(8)  = 16
dbl(9)  = 18
dbl(10) = 20
```

11. INDEPENDENT COMPILATION

C compilers support independent compilation, that is, they allow parts of a program to be compiled independently of each other. The unit of compilation of a C program is the file. Large programs should be partitioned into several files for ease of manipulation and compilation. If this is done, then when the program is modified, only the files that have been affected by the modification will need to be recompiled. The whole program need not be recompiled. Compiling an entire program every time it is modified, especially if the program is large, can be very time consuming.

To produce an executable version of a program, each file containing parts of the program is compiled to produce an object file. These object files are then linked together, with appropriate libraries, such as the standard and math libraries, to produce an executable version of the program.

As far as possible, programs should be designed as collections of small functions. Related definitions, declarations, and function bodies should be stored in the same file, but to minimize the recompilation effort, the files should be kept as small as possible.

For details about how to invoke the compiler and linker, please refer to your C compiler manual.

12. INTERRUPT (SIGNAL) HANDLING

Pascal does not provide any facility for interrupt handling. On the other hand, C supports signal (interrupt) handling by means of the *signal* function. Although signal handling is not part of K&R C, it is likely to be included in ANSI C. Most UNIX system C compilers provide this function and it is also provided by the Lattice C [Latt86] compiler. To set up an interrupt trap, function *signal* is called with two arguments: the signal (interrupt type) *sig*, and the name of the trap function *f* that is to be invoked when this signal is trapped. As its result, *signal* returns the previous trap function for the specified signal. There are two special interrupt handling functions: *SIG_IGN* which specifies that the signal is to be ignored and *SIG_DFL* which specifies that default action is to be taken when the signal is caught.

The Lattice C compiler supports only two signals: *SIGFPE* which is raised when a floating point error occurs and *SIGINT* which is raised whenever the user types control-C or control-break. See your C compiler reference manual for details about the *signal* function and its use. Note that the *signal* function is often used in conjunction with the *setjmp* and *longjmp* functions (not discussed in this book).

As an example of the use of *signal*, consider the following program that prints the positive numbers starting from 0. The user can terminate the program anytime by typing control-C and then answering affirmatively to the program's query; a negative response will cause the program to continue printing:

```
#include <signal.h>
#include <stdio.h>

FILE *fp;   /*fp must be a global variable*/

int quit()
{
    int c;
    printf("you really want to quit? (y or n):");
    if ((c = getchar()) == 'y' || c == 'Y')
        exit(0);
    while (getchar() != '\n');
    signal(SIGINT, quit);
}
main()
{
    int i;

    signal(SIGINT, quit);
    for(i=0;;i++) printf("%d\n", i);
}
```

The *signal* function is first called in *main* to set up the signal handler function *quit* and then again, if necessary, in *quit* itself to reset the signal trapping.

13. PROGRAM TERMINATION

Pascal programs terminate by completing execution of the program. However, C programs can terminate in three different ways: by completing execution of the *main* function, by calling the *exit* function, or by executing the *return* statement in the *main* function.

Function *exit* closes all open files. It also cleans the output buffers causing the buffered items to be written to the appropriate files. (Calling function *_exit* terminates the program without closing the files and without writing the output buffers.) *exit* is called with a zero argument to indicate successful (normal) termination and with a non-zero argument to indicate error (abnormal) termination.

14. ACCESSING OPERATING SYSTEM FACILITIES

Unlike standard Pascal, C provides the library function *system* which can be used to execute any command of the underlying operating system. For example, the calls

```
system("cls"); system("show 1");
```

will clear the screen by executing the MS-DOS command "cls" and then run the user program *show* with the argument 1. Note that a complete path name specifying the command to be executed can also be given as an argument to *system*. The *system* command returns −1 if the specified command could not be executed.

15. CALLING ROUTINES WRITTEN IN OTHER LANGUAGES

Most C compilers provide facilities for calling routines written in high-level languages such as FORTRAN and Pascal. Machine language functions can also be called from C programs. Calling such functions is just like calling ordinary C functions. Of course, for a machine language function to be called from a C program, it must be written according to the conventions used by the C compiler. For example, machine language functions must follow the C compiler's convention for storing the arguments and the return address on the stack. Details of these conventions should be in the manual describing the C compiler. (Note that your C compiler may also provide an option instructing it to generate assembly language code. You may be able to use the assembly code generated for a C function to determine the conventions used by your C compiler to generate code for a C function and then pattern your machine language function on this code.)

16. EXAMPLES

16.1 A GENERAL PURPOSE SWAP ROUTINE

Consider the problem of writing a function *swap* that exchanges the values of two variables of any type including derived types such as arrays and structures. There are two problems that must be solved:

- C function argument types must match the parameter types. So how can arguments of arbitrary types be passed to the *swap* function?

- Arguments to be exchanged will be of different sizes depending upon their type and, in case of arrays, the number of array dimensions and their sizes. How do we know how many elements of an array to swap? In other words, how do we determine the argument size?

The first problem is solved by defining *swap* to accept character pointers specifying the addresses of the objects to be swapped; this requires that the user convert the object addresses to character pointers when calling *swap*. The second problem is solved by incorporating a third argument that specifies the argument size. (Note that it is not possible to write such a *swap* function in Pascal primarily because Pascal does not provide facilities for converting between arbitrary pointer types and for determining the storage occupied by the program objects.)

Here is the general *swap* function:

```
void swap(a, b, n)
    char *a, *b;
    int n;
{
    char tmp;

    while(n-- >0) {
        tmp = *(a+n);
        *(a+n) = *(b+n);
        *(b+n) = tmp;
    }
}
```

Pointers *a* and *b* must refer to the beginning of the objects to be swapped. Function *swap* swaps the objects by exchanging the storage occupied by them one byte at a time.

Here are some variable definitions and some sample calls to *swap*:

```
typedef struct {
    char *name[MAX];
    int age;
} employee;

employee a, b;
char x[MAX], y[MAX];
char *s, *t;
...
swap((char *)&s, (char *)&t, 1);
swap(x, y, MAX);
swap((char *) &a, (char *) &b, sizeof(employee));
```

Strings implemented as pointers can be swapped by just exchanging the values of the pointers. Alternatively, instead of swapping pointer values, elements of the two strings can be physically exchanged:

```
swap(s, t, MAX);
```

Unlike arrays implemented using pointers, explicitly defined arrays cannot be swapped by just exchanging pointer values because array names are constant pointers whose values cannot be changed.

16.2 SORTING

Sorting is probably the single most important computer activity. Consequently, it is important to design efficient sorting routines. We will show you two different sorting programs: bubble sort and shell sort. Shell sort is a variation of bubble or interchange sort that, on the average, performs much better than bubble sort.

Bubble sort works as follows: assume that the left part of array a, up to and including element $a[i]$, has been sorted. (Initially, the sorted part of the array consists of only element $a[0]$.) Element $a[i+1]$, whose value is x, is now interchanged with adjacent elements on the left until the left part of the array up to and including element $a[i+1]$, whose value may now not be x, are in order. This process is repeated until the whole array is sorted.

Here is function *bubble* (stored in file *bubble.c*) that sorts an array of integers in increasing order:

```
void sort(a, n)
    int a[], n;
{
    int i, j, tmp;

    for (i=1; i<n; i++)
        for (j=i-1; j>=0 && a[j]>a[j+1]; j--) {
            tmp = a[j];
            a[j] = a[j+1];
            a[j+1] = tmp;
        }
}
```

Bubble sort is not very efficient because every time the left part of the array is to be extended with a new element, on the average a large number of interchanges are required to shift the new element into position. Shell sort orders the array in several passes. In the first pass, instead of comparing adjacent elements, it compares and exchanges elements separated by $d-1$ elements. With each successive pass, d is reduced until eventually, for the last pass, it equals 1 (i.e., adjacent elements are compared and exchanged). The idea is that elements that are grossly out of position will be interchanged in the earlier passes which do not require so many interchanges. The last pass is exactly like bubble sort, but the hope is that very few elements will need to be interchanged in the last pass.

Here is function *shellsort* (stored in *shell.c*) that sorts an array of integers in increasing order [Kern78]:

```
void shellsort(a, n)
    int a[], n;
{
    int i, j, tmp, d;

    for (d = n/2; d>0; d = d/2)
        for (i=d; i<n; i++)
            for (j=i-d; j>=0&&a[j]>a[j+d]; j=j-d){
                tmp = a[j];
                a[j] = a[j+d];
                a[j+d] = tmp;
            }
}
```

16.3 QUEUES

A *queue* is a data structure which is used to implement the first-in-first-out
(FIFO) discipline. The first element inserted into a queue is the first
element that will be removed from the queue. Here are functions for
interfacing with a queue of integers:

empty() If the queue is empty, return non-zero; otherwise, zero.

full()   If the queue is full, return non-zero; otherwise, zero.

add(x)   Add element *x* to the queue. If successful, return non-zero;
           otherwise, zero.

get(p)   Store the first element of the queue in **p*. This element is
           then removed from the queue. If successful, return non-
           zero; otherwise, zero.

Now here are the declarations of the functions implementing the queue data
structure (stored in file *queue.h*):

```
int empty(), full(), add(), get();
```

Here are the definitions of variables and of functions implementing the queue
data structure (stored in file *queue.c*):

```
#include "queue.h"

#define N 128
static int a[N], in = 0, out = 0, n = 0;

int empty() {return n == 0;}
int full()  {return n == N;}

int add(x)
    int x;
{
    if (full())
        return 0;
    a[in] = x; in = (in+1) % N;
    n++;
    return 1;
}

int get(p)
    int *p;
{
    if (empty())
        return 0;
    *p = a[in]; out = (out+1) % N;
    n--;
    return 1;
}
```

Notice the use of static global variables for communication between functions.

16.4 PAGINATOR

To illustrate how command-line arguments can be given to a C program, we will write a paginator program, that is, a program that displays a file on the screen one page at a time. The file to be displayed with the pagination program, called *pager*, is supplied as an argument:

pager *file*

By default, *pager* assumes the page length to be 24 lines. An alternative page length can be supplied as the second command-line argument when invoking *pager*:

pager *file page-length*

Here is the *pager* program (stored in file *pager.c*):

```
#include <stdio.h>
#define LL 132
#define PL 24

/*page length can be supplied a: the second*/
/*argument on the command line*/
main(argc, argv)
  int argc; char *argv[];
{
  char line[LL+1];
  int n, pl = PL;
  FILE *fp;

  if ((fp = fopen(argv[1], "r")) == NULL) {
    printf("error, cannot open file %s\n",argv[1]);
    exit(1);
  }
  if (argc == 3)
    sscanf(argv[2], "%d", &pl);

  n = 0;
  while (fgets(line, LL, fp) != NULL) {
    if (n++ < pl)
      printf("%s", line);
    else {
      printf("\033[7mType enter for more:\033[0m");
      while (getchar() != '\n')
        ;
      printf("%s", line);
      n = 1;
    }
  }
  fclose(fp);
}
```

17. EXERCISES

1. Implement the queue functions of the example given in the last section without using global variables. Compare the two solutions.

2. Compare the Pascal approach of providing a facility to pass parameters by reference, i.e., *var* parameters, with the C approach of using pointers to simulate passing arguments by reference.

3. Compare the efficiency of bubble sort and shell sort by analyzing the number of comparisons and exchanges required to sort large samples of data. Modify the bubble and shell sort programs to count the comparisons and exchanges.

4. Write a general sorting routine *gsort* that can sort arrays with any type of elements. Function *gsort* will be called with the following arguments:

    a. A pointer to the first element of the array (of type *char *).
    b. Number of elements in the array.
    c. Size of the array elements.
    d. Pointer to a function for comparing two array elements.

Suppose the array elements are of type *employee*:

```
typedef struct {
    char *name;
    int id;
} employee;
```

The comparison function for sorting the array according to employee id may be written as

```
int lt(a, b)   /*a less than b*/
    char *a, *b;
{
    employee *p = (employee *) a,
             *q = (employee *) b;

    return p->id < q->id ? 1 : 0;
}
```

5. Write a function *max* that computes the maximum element of a floating point array. Test it by writing a *main* function that defines and initializes an array, calls *max* with the array as an argument, and then prints the maximum value in the array.

CHAPTER 6

POINTERS

C pointers are used to directly access memory locations (a pointer value is a memory address). Only meaningful or valid pointer values should be used to access memory. Otherwise, you will get garbage when reading memory, and by writing to these addresses, you may destroy the program or the program data, or you may update the system information causing the operating system to crash. Valid C pointer values are those that refer to dynamically allocated storage, and when allowed, addresses of variables and memory locations reserved for hardware devices. Some computer systems do not allow users to access all parts of memory. For example, the region of memory containing the operating system code and data may be out of bounds for users. Attempts to access invalid or prohibited addresses can cause program termination. Accessing memory using a null pointer value can also cause program termination.

Although pointers are a very powerful programming tool, it is relatively easy to make errors when using them. Consequently, pointers are a source of many programming errors and they should therefore be used with great care. This is especially important because errors caused by pointers are hard to discover, for their effects do not become apparent until long after the errors have occurred.

1. ALLOCATING & DEALLOCATING STORAGE

In C, as in Pascal, objects can be freely created and referenced at run time by allocating an appropriate amount of storage, assigning the address of the storage to a pointer variable and then referencing the object with the pointer. The only limitation on the number of objects that can be created at run time is the total amount of available memory.

Storage is allocated from an area of memory called the *heap*, which is reserved for allocating storage for run-time objects. Each C compiler provides a set of functions for allocating storage from the heap and freeing (deallocating) storage, that is, returning previously allocated storage to the heap.

Here is a brief description of the C storage allocation and deallocation functions:

malloc(n)   Allocate *n* bytes of storage. If successful, *malloc* returns a character pointer to the allocated storage. Otherwise, *malloc* returns the null pointer *NULL*. *malloc* is the storage allocation function that is used most often.

calloc(nelem, elemsize)   Allocate *nelem*elemsize* bytes of storage. *calloc* is like *malloc* but it sets all the bits of the allocated storage to zero.

realloc(ptr, n)   Change the size of a previously allocated storage region that begins at address *ptr* to *n* while ensuring that the storage contents are preserved. If necessary, a new block of memory is allocated; in this case the contents of the old memory block specified by *ptr* are copied to the new memory block, and the old memory block is deallocated. *realloc* returns a pointer to the (possibly new) *n*-byte block of memory. If reallocation is not possible, then *realloc* returns *NULL*.

free(ptr)   Free (deallocate) previously allocated storage that begins at the address specified by *ptr* and returns it to the heap. *free* returns 0 if it is successful; otherwise, it returns –1.

The above storage allocation functions are often collectively referred to as "storage allocators."

Some C compilers provide a header file containing the declarations of the storage allocation and deallocation functions. For example, the Lattice C compiler provides the header file *stdlib.h* that contains declarations of these functions. If such a header file is not provided by your compiler, then you will have to explicitly declare these functions before using them. See Appendix 1 for a detailed description of these functions.

Here is an example of the commonly used programming paradigm for allocating storage using *malloc*:

```
#include <stdio.h>   /*contains defn. of NULL*/
#include <stdlib.h>
employee *pe;
  ...
if ((pe = (employee *) malloc(sizeof(employee)))
                                == NULL) {
```
print error message and/or perform error action
```
}
```

As shown above, when using a storage allocator, it is important to check whether or not the storage requested was allocated. The *sizeof* operator is frequently used to determine the amount of storage required. Note that because *malloc* (and the other storage allocators) return a character pointer, it may be necessary to cast the pointer to the right pointer type before assigning it to a variable. In this example, the value returned by *malloc* is cast to "*employee* *", that is, "pointer to *employee*".

2. POINTER ARITHMETIC

C allows you to add an integer to and subtract an integer from a pointer, and subtract one pointer from another. Other arithmetic operations on pointers, such as adding or multiplying two pointers, are not allowed. The effect of adding an integer i to a pointer p which points to objects of type T is to add the value $i*sizeof(T)$ to p; that is, the value added is the number of bytes occupied by i objects of type T. To add the integer value i, and not the space occupied by i objects of type T, casts must be used, for example,

```
p = (T *) ((int) p + i);
```

Similarly, the effect of subtracting an integer i from a pointer p, which points to objects of type T, is to subtract the value $i*sizeof(T)$ from p.

When subtracting one pointer from another, say p from q, both pointers being of the same type T, then the result is the number of items of type T that can be fitted in the memory between p and q. The result can be converted to bytes by multiplying it by $sizeof(T)$.

3. LISTS: AN EXAMPLE OF POINTER USE

After arrays, lists are probably the most important data structures in programming. In fact, there are languages like LISP which are built with the list type, and not the array type as in many languages, as the primary data structure.

Lists are typically implemented in C, as in Pascal, by using pointers. A pointer to the first element of the list is always kept. This pointer, called the *list head*, is used for accessing the list. A null list head, by convention, indicates that the list is empty.

Each element of the list is implemented with a structure that conceptually consists of two parts: the first part is a set of components for storing information, and the second part is a pointer that points to the next element in the list. A null pointer value signals the end of the list.

Lists of the type described above are called *singly-linked* lists because there is only one pointer (link) from one element to the next. Using this pointer, the list can be traversed in one direction: you can go from one list element to the next element but not to the previous element. Other types of lists such as *doubly-linked* lists, allow list traversal in both directions: forward to the next element and back to the previous element. In doubly-linked lists two pointers must be kept: one for the next element and one for the previous element.

Building lists is straightforward. You start with the list head and insert a new element at an appropriate place in the list, for instance, you can insert it at the beginning of the list, in the middle of the list, or at the end of the list. Before we show you the code to do this, here are some declarations and definitions that we will use:

```
typedef struct elem {
    char name[MAX];
    struct elem *next;
} elem;

elem *h = NULL, *p;   /*h is the list head*/
                      /*p is a temporary ptr*/
char name[MAX];
```

Here is some code to allocate an element, to assign values to it and to insert it at the beginning of the list pointed to by *h*:

```
if ((p = (elem *) malloc(sizeof(elem)))==NULL) {
    puts("not enough heap storage");
    exit(1);
}
strcpy(p->name, name);
p->next = h;
h = p;
```

The last two instructions are the ones which actually insert the element pointed by *p* in the list pointed by *h*. These two instructions should usually be encapsulated in a function, such as *add*, which can be called, for example, as *add(&h, p)*. Notice that the address of *h*, not its value, must be passed to *add*, because function *add* may change the value of *h*. Here is the definition of function *add*:

```
void add(h, p)
    elem **h, *p;
{
    p->next = *h;
    *h = p;
}
```

Encapsulating the code for list insertion in a function such as *add* will facilitate making changes to the insertion strategy. Only the definition of this function may need to be changed instead of all the places where an element is inserted in a list.

Processing list elements, for example, printing all the list elements, requires stepping through the list sequentially one element at a time. Here is code for printing all the list elements:

```
for(p = h; p != NULL; p = p->next)
    printf("%s\n", p->name);
```

Unlike an array, a list is a sequential data structure. An arbitrary element of an array can be accessed with its subscript but accessing an arbitrary list element requires starting from the list head. For example, accessing the last element of a list requires starting with the list head and stepping, using the pointer to the next list element, through all the list elements. Lists also require more storage than arrays. Unlike arrays, lists need to keep pointers for list traversal. The extra storage required for singly-linked lists is one word (that is, the size of a pointer) per list element.

Having mentioned some disadvantages of lists, it is now time to mention some advantages of lists. Unlike arrays, lists can grow in size until you run out of storage. In many languages, including Pascal, the array size is fixed; once the array has been allocated, its size cannot be changed. (Note that C is one of the few languages in which an array size can be changed, by using the function *realloc*, provided the array is implemented using pointers and dynamically allocated storage. However, increasing the array size may require copying the existing array elements into a new region of memory. This array copying can be an expensive proposition, especially if the array involved is large and if it is done often.)

Unlike in the case of an array, items can be inserted in a list between any two elements without requiring that adjacent elements be shifted, and any element can be deleted without creating a gap in the list. Inserting an item into a list or deleting an item from a list requires only a few operations.

If a list is initially sorted, then this ordering of the list elements can be preserved if every new element is added between an appropriate pair of list elements. For example, when inserting a new element in a list sorted in increasing order, the new element should be added after an element less than or equal to the new element, but before an element greater than it. Lists can also be implemented with arrays by using subscripts to simulate pointers. However, such lists will not be as flexible as lists implemented using pointers. For example, in many languages it may not be possible to make the lists grow beyond the initial size of the array. This is not a problem in C, because as mentioned above, array sizes can be increased dynamically.

4. POINTERS & ARRAYS

In C, there is a very strong relationship between pointers and arrays (and therefore strings). Arrays can be treated as pointers and vice versa. In many ways, arrays are primarily a convenient mechanism for manipulating pointers. Suppose a is declared as a character array. Then the ith element of array a is accessed using the array element notation $a[i]$. An array name is also a pointer to the first element of the array. For example, the array name a can be thought of as a character pointer that points to the first element of a, that is, it points to the beginning of the storage allocated for a. Therefore, the ith element of a can also be accessed as $*(a+i)$. Similarly, any pointer value can be thought of as the name of an array that begins at the address specified by the pointer value. As an example, suppose that p is a character pointer that has been initialized properly. Then the ith byte of storage, relative to the address pointed to by i, can be referenced as $p[i]$. In general, if p is a pointer of type T, then $p[i]$ refers to the ith block of storage of size $sizeof(T)$ beginning from p.

Because array elements can be accessed using pointers and the storage referenced by a pointer accessed as array elements, C has no way of knowing whether or not a user is referring to a valid array element. Consequently, unlike Pascal, the C run-time system will not give a "subscript-out-of-range" error when a negative array subscript or a positive subscript greater than the upper array bound is encountered. A C array (or pointer) can, in effect, be used to access any element of accessible memory.

Strictly speaking, C can flag a subscript error for array elements accessed using the array subscript notation. One reason why C compilers do not check for invalid array subscripts is that array subscript checking is expensive. In general, it must be done at run time and this slows program execution. Recognizing the importance of subscript checking, at least in the program debugging phase, some C debugging tools such as C interpreters now check for invalid subscripts.

To illustrate the close relationship between arrays and pointers, we will write a pointer version of the function *left* that returns an *n*-character prefix of a string. The array version of *left*, which was given in Chapter 2, is shown below for your convenience:

```
void left(s, n, d) /*set d to the leftmost n*/
                   /*characters of s*/
    char s[]; int n; char d[];
{
    int i;

    if (n > strlen(s))
        strcpy(d, s);
    else {
        for (i=0; i<n; i++)
            d[i] = s[i];
        d[i] = '\0';
    }
}
```

Now here is the equivalent pointer version (stored in file *leftp.c*):

```
void left(s, n, d) /*set d to the leftmost n*/
                   /*characters of s*/
    char *s; int n; char *d;
{
    char *p;

    if (n > strlen(s))
        strcpy(d, s);
    else {
        p = d;
        while (n-- > 0)
            *p++ = *s++;
        *p = '\0';
    }
}
```

The *while* loop shown above could also have been written as the following *for* loop with a null body:

```
for(; n--; *p++ = *s++)
    ;
```

There is one difference between array names and pointers. An array name is a constant; its value cannot be changed. On the other hand, a pointer name is a variable whose value can be changed. As an example illustrating this difference, consider two strings defined as

```
char s[MAX], t[MAX];
```

whose values we want to exchange by calling function *swaps*:

```
void swaps(a, b)
   char **a, **b;
{
   char *tmp;

   tmp = *a; *a = *b; *b = tmp;
}
```

Function *swaps* takes two pointers, of type pointer to character, as arguments and exchanges the strings pointed to by them. Calling *swaps* with the addresses of pointers *s* and *t*, which are character pointers, as in

```
swaps(&s, &t);   /*&s and &t are pointers to*/
                 /*character pointers*/
```

is illegal because *s* and *t* are constants and extracting the address of a constant is not allowed. (Your compiler may not flag this as an error but you will most likely get garbage). On the other hand, had *s* and *t* had been declared as character pointers and storage allocated for them dynamically by calling a storage allocator such as *malloc*, as shown below, then the call *swaps(&s, &t)* would be legal and it would exchange the values of the *s* and *t*:

```
char *s, *t;
   ...

if ((s = malloc(MAX)) == NULL) {
   fprintf(stderr, "not enough heap storage\n");
   exit(1);
}
if ((t = malloc(MAX)) == NULL) {
   fprintf(stderr, "not enough heap storage\n");
   exit(1);
}
   ...
swap(&s, &t);
```

Of course, an alternative version of *swaps* that exchanges the two strings by swapping individual characters can be used with strings implemented with explicitly defined arrays. However, in general, this will be relatively inefficient because it will require many more exchanges than just exchanging the pointer values as shown above.

5. DYNAMIC ARRAYS

Like Pascal, C does not provide an explicit mechanism for specifying *dynamic arrays*, that is, arrays whose sizes can be specified at run time. However, dynamic arrays can easily be implemented in C by using pointers. Allocating a dynamic array is a two-step process: first a pointer variable is defined and then it is set to point to explicitly allocated storage. Remember that array names are really pointers (of type pointer to array element type). As an example, suppose we want to allocate an *n*-element integer array, where *n* is an arbitrary expression such as a parameter value. Using the storage allocator *malloc*, storage of size *n*sizeof(int)* is allocated and its address assigned to *a*:

```
int *a;
...
if ((a=(int *) malloc(n * sizeof(int)))==NULL) {
    fprintf(stderr, "not enough heap storage\n");
    exit(1);
}
```

Function *malloc* takes as its argument the number of bytes to be allocated, which in our case is *n* times the size of each array element. It returns a pointer of type character to the block of storage allocated by it. This pointer must be converted to the desired pointer type which, in the case of this example, is an integer pointer. The type conversion is specified with the cast "*(int *)*".

Now this dynamic array with the name *a* can be used just like explicitly defined arrays; for instance, you can reference element *i* of array *a* as *a[i]*.

Allocating 2-dimensional arrays is similar. The storage must be allocated for the total number of elements in the array and the array elements are referenced using the standard notation, for example, *p[i][j]*, where *p* is the pointer that points to the beginning of the allocated storage.

5.1 ERASING ARRAYS

Arrays implemented by using pointers and explicitly allocated storage can be "erased", that is, the storage used for these arrays can be deallocated by calling function *free*. The freed storage will be reused automatically by the storage allocation functions. Note that just assigning a new value to a pointer without freeing the storage pointed by it may mean that this storage will be lost for the duration of the program.

6. EXAMPLES

6.1 DETERMINING THE AMOUNT OF STORAGE AVAILABLE FOR DYNAMIC ALLOCATION

Here is a program that determines the amount of storage that can be dynamically allocated, that is, the size of the heap (stored in file *memsize.c*):

```
#include <stdio.h>
#include <stdlib.h>
#define N 1024   /*1 Kilobyte*/
main()
{
    int n = 0;

    while (malloc(N) != NULL)
        n++;
    printf("Dynamic Storage = %d Kbytes\n", n);
}
```

Note that the size of the heap depends upon the hardware configuration, the size of the operating system, and the size of the program.

6.2 USING LISTS TO MANIPULATE STUDENT RECORDS

In this example, we will write a set of functions to implement and manipulate a list of student records. Each student record contains the student's name, id, and grade point average. Student records are kept in a file, ordered by student id. For fast interaction, the records are read into memory and stored in a list. The ordering of the student records is preserved in the presence of any additions to and deletions from the list. After the list updates have been completed, the student records are written, ordered by student id, back to the file.

The following list manipulation functions are to be implemented:

readlist(db, ps)   Read student records from the file *db* into a list whose header is stored in pointer *ps*; if successful, *readlist* returns 1; otherwise, 0.

writelist(db, ps)   Store the student records from the list pointed to by *ps*, maintaining the order in which they appear in the list, in the file *db*. If successful, *writelist* returns 1; otherwise, 0.

add(ps, p)   Add the student record pointed to by *p* to the list pointed to by *ps*. The list must remain ordered by student id. If successful, *add* returns 1; otherwise, 0.

remove(ps, id)   Remove from the list pointed to by *ps*, the student record with identification number *id*, if there is such a record; otherwise, do nothing.

in(ps, id)   Check to see if a student record with identification number *id* is in the list pointed to by *ps*. If such a record is present, then *in* returns a pointer to this record; otherwise, *NULL*.

The following declarations, kept in the header file *student.h*, will be used by the student list functions:

```
#include <stdio.h>
#include <string.h>
#include <stdlib.h>

#define NAMELEN 32
#define STDSIZE (int) sizeof(student)

typedef struct student {
    char first, last[NAMELEN];
    int id;
    float gpa;
    struct student *next;
} student;

student *in();
int readlist(), writelist(), add();
void remove();
```

Here is the definition of function *readlist* (stored in file *stread.c*):

```
#include "student.h"
int readlist(db, ps)
   char *db;
   student **ps;
{
    student *p, *last;
    FILE *fp;
    int none = 1;

    *ps = NULL;
    if ((fp = fopen(db,"r")) == NULL) {
        printf("cannot open file %s\n", db);
        return 0;
    }
    if ((p=(student *) malloc(STDSIZE))==NULL){
        puts("not enough heap storage\n");
        fclose(fp);
        return 0;
    }
    while(fread((char *) p,STDSIZE,1,fp)==1){
        if (none)
            {*ps = last = p; none = 0;}
        else
            {last->next = p; last = p;}
        if ((p=(student *) malloc(STDSIZE))==NULL){
            puts("not enough heap storage\n");
            fclose(fp);
            return 0;
        }
    }
    if (!none) last->next = NULL;
    free((char *)p);
    fclose(fp);
    if (ferror(fp))
        return 0;
    else
        return 1;
}
```

File reading is terminated upon encountering an end of file or upon encountering an error. Function *ferror* is used to distinguish between these two cases.

Here is the definition of function *writelist* (stored in file *stwrite.c*):

```
#include "student.h"
int writelist (db, ps)
    char *db;
    student *ps;
{
    FILE *fp;

    if ((fp = fopen(db,"w")) == NULL) {
        printf("cannot open file %s\n", db);
        return 0;
    }
    for (; ps != NULL; ps = ps->next)
        if (fwrite((char *) ps,STDSIZE,1,fp)!=1){
            printf("write error on file %s\n",db);
            fclose(fp);
            return 0;
        }
    fclose(fp);
    return 1;
}
```

Function *writelist* writes the records into the file according to the order in which they appear in the list.

Here is the definition of function *add* (stored in file *stadd.c*):

```
#include "student.h"
int add(ps, p)
     /*adds elements while keeping list sorted*/
   student **ps, *p;
          /*ps is address of pointer to list */
          /*head p is to be added*/
{
   student *a, *b;

   if (in(*ps, p->id)) {
       printf("duplicate entry for d = %d,
              name = %c %s\n",
              p->id, p->first, p->last);
       printf("entry not added\n");
       return 0;
   }
   if ((a=(student *) malloc(STDSIZE))==NULL){
       puts("not enough heap storage\n");
       return 0;
   }
   a->first = p->first;
   strcpy(a->last, p->last);
   a->id = p->id;
   a->gpa = p->gpa;

   if (*ps == NULL || (*ps)->id > p->id) {
                    /*add at head of list*/
       a->next = *ps;
       *ps = a;
       return 1;
   }
   for(b = *ps; b->next != NULL &&
           (b->next)->id < p->id; b = b->next)
       ;  /*find element after which to add p*/
   a->next = b->next; b->next = a;
   return 1;
}
```

A new element *s* is inserted between two elements such that the element before *s* has a smaller *id* than *s* and the element after it has a greater *id*. (The assumption here is that the list elements are kept sorted in increasing order.)

Here is the definition of function *remove* (stored in file *stremove.c*):

```
#include "student.h"
void remove(ps, id)
    student **ps; /*pointer to the list head*/
    int id;   /*id entry is to be removed*/
{
    student *last, *cur;

    if (*ps == NULL)
        return;
    if ((*ps)->id == id) {
        free((char *) *ps);
        *ps = (*ps)->next;
        return;
    }
    for (last=*ps, cur=(*ps)->next; cur!=NULL;
         last=cur, cur=cur->next)
        if (cur->id == id) {
            last->next = cur->next;
            free((char *) cur);
            return;
        }
}
```

Finally, here is the definition of function *in* (stored in file *stin.c*):

```
#include "student.h"
student *in(ps, id)
    student *ps; /*ps is the list head*/
    int id;      /*id entry is to be removed*/
{
    student *p;

    for (p = ps; p != NULL; p = p->next)
        if (p->id == id)
            return p;
        else if (p->id > id)
            return NULL;
    return NULL;
}
```

To illustrate how these functions are used, we will use them to write a small application: a program to answer student queries about their current grade point average. With this program, students can use a specially designated terminal to determine their latest grade point average, much like the way customers at a bank can use a terminal to determine their latest account balance. To make it difficult for students to determine the grade point averages of other students, we will require students to enter both their ids and their last names. The grade point average will be shown only if the entered student id and name match.

Assuming that the student database is stored in file *student.db*, here is the grade point average query program (stored in file *student.c*):

```
#include "student.h"
char db[] = "student.db";
main()
{
    student *ps, *s;
            /*ps points to head of student list*/
            /*s is a temporary variable*/
    int id, c; char last[NAMELEN];

    if (readlist("student.db", &ps) == 0)
        puts("error, cannot set up student list");
    for (;;) {
        printf("type id & press enter:");
        if (scanf("%d", &id) == EOF)
            exit(0);
        while((c=getchar()) !='\n');
                            /*skip rest of line*/
        printf("type last name & press enter:");
        if (c == EOF)
            exit(1);
        gets(last);
        if (((s = in(ps, id)) != NULL) &&
                    strcmp(last, s->last) == 0){
            printf("your GPA is %g\n", s->gpa);
            puts("PRESS ENTER TO CLEAR SCREEN\n");
            while((c=getchar()) !='\n');
                            /*skip rest of line*/
            puts("\033[2J");
                    /*clear screen; see [IBM83b]*/
        }
        else
            puts("invalid name & id combination");
    }
}
```

The program will terminate upon encountering an end of file, that is, when a control-Z followed by carriage return is typed on MS-DOS systems (on UNIX systems, an end of file is indicated by typing control-D).

6.3 TREES

Trees are dynamic data structures that are similar to lists. In fact, lists can be considered to be a "degenerate" case of trees. Unlike a list element, each tree element (node) can have several successors. We shall restrict our discussion to *binary* trees in which an element can have at most two successors: these successors are often called the left and right successors. A tree element that has no successors is called a *leaf*. The pointer that points to the first element of a tree is called the *root* of the tree.

Ordered binary trees are a special class of binary trees which are constructed according to the following ordering rule: the information component (such as the student id) of the left successor of a node *n* precedes (e.g., is less than) the information component of *n*, which in turn precedes the information component of its right successor. Ordered binary trees are used to speed up searches.

To process (access) information stored at all nodes of a tree, the tree elements must be accessed in some order. Here are three commonly used "tree traversal" strategies:

Preorder   Access the left subtree, then the current node, and then the right subtree.

Inorder   Access the current node, then the left subtree, and then the right subtree.

Postorder Access the right subtree, then the current node, and then the left subtree.

The above accessing strategies are defined recursively. Recursion is a very natural tool for processing all the elements of a tree.

To illustrate binary tree manipulation, we will write two functions: *add* to insert a node into an ordered binary tree, and *print* to print the information components of all the tree nodes in preorder fashion.

First, here is the header file that contains the declaration of a tree node (stored in file *tree.h*):

```
#include <stdio.h>
typedef struct node {
    int i;
    struct node *left, *right;
} node;
void print(), add();
```

Here is function *add* (stored in file *tadd.c*):

```c
#include "tree.h"
void add(proot, i)
    node **proot;
    int i;
{
    node *n, *p = *proot;

    if ((n=(node *) malloc(sizeof(node)))==NULL){
        puts("not enough heap storage");
        exit(1);
    }
    n->i = i; n->left = NULL; n->right = NULL;

    if (*proot == NULL) {
        *proot = n;
        return;
    }
    for (;;)
        if (n->i < p->i) {
            if (p->left == NULL)
                {p->left = n; return;}
            else
                p = p->left;
        }
        else if (n->i > p->i) {
            if (p->right == NULL)
                {p->right = n; return;}
            else
                p = p->right;
        }
        else
            return;
}
```

Here is function *print* (stored in file *tprint.c*):

```
#include "tree.h"

void print(root)
    node *root;
{
    if (root == NULL)
        return;
    else {
        print(root->left);
        printf("%d\n", root->i);
        print(root->right);
    }
}
```

6.4 PRINTING THE CALL STACK

The ability to access specific locations in memory is essential for systems programming. Pointers facilitate access to specific memory locations. As an example, suppose a systems programmer wants to print a portion of the "call stack" for debugging. When any function is called (including *main*, which is the first function to be called), the function arguments and the function variables are allocated in an array on top of the items of the function containing the call. This array is called a *stack* because the last items allocated on the stack will be the first ones to be deallocated (the last function call must be completed before the previous one). In most languages, you cannot examine the call stack dynamically. But in C you can use pointers to print the data in the call stack.

To print the top portion of the stack, we will write a print function *prntstk* that takes the address of its first parameter and prints memory locations surrounding it. By making this function have more than one parameter and calling it with easily recognizable values, we will be able to quickly identify the values on the stack.

Here is a program that prints part of the call stack (stored in file *callstk.c*):

```
#include "stdio.h"
#define N 5

/*prnstk: test routine to print part of the */
/*        call stack; N elements below the  */
/*        address where the first parameter */
/*        is placed, and N elements starting*/
/*        with the first parameter address  */
void prntstk(a, b, c)
    int a, b, c;
{
    int d = -8;
    int *p;
    for (p = &a-N; p < &a+N; p++)
        printf("addr=0x%x,val=%d\n",(int) p,*p);
}

main()
{
    prntstk(-5, -6, -7);
}
```

The output produced by the above program (when compiled with the Lattice
C compiler) is shown below:

```
addr=0xa86,val=66
addr=0xa88,val=-8
addr=0xa8a,val=2698
addr=0xa8c,val=2710
addr=0xa8e,val=930
addr=0xa90,val=-5
addr=0xa92,val=-6
addr=0xa94,val=-7
addr=0xa96,val=2720
addr=0xa98,val=1069
```

The negative values assigned to variable *d* and to the parameters *a*, *b*, and *c*
make it very easy to identify their locations on the call stack. Some of the
other locations contain information such as hardware register values at the
time of the call and the function return address (the address of the code to
be executed after returning from the function).

7. EXERCISES

1. What are the pros and cons of using singly-linked lists versus doubly-linked lists?

2. Modify the tree printing algorithm to print the information components of the tree nodes in postorder.

3. What are the problems involved in deleting a tree node? Write a function to delete a binary tree node.

4. Suppose your implementation does not provide the storage allocation function *malloc* and the deallocation function *free*. How will you implement *malloc* and *free*? (Hint: Use a large global static array.) What will you do with the freed storage? Will you keep the freed storage as separate blocks for later reallocation or will you combine it with other free blocks, if possible, to build a larger free block?

CHAPTER 7

C PREPROCESSOR

The C preprocessor, as its name indicates, processes the C program before it is compiled; it is automatically invoked by the C compiler. The preprocessor transforms the program as specified by the preprocessor instructions given in the program. These instructions, which are different from C instructions, begin in column one with the # character. Note that all other instructions in the program should normally be C code (or should lead to C code after preprocessing). However, as far as the C preprocessor is concerned, these lines can be arbitrary sequences of characters. Except for constant definitions, Pascal does not have the counterparts of the facilities provided by the C preprocessor.

The C preprocessor is an integral part of the C programming environment. Many C facilities are implemented as C preprocessor macros, for example, definitions of constants such as *EOF* and *NULL*, input routines such as *getchar*, the various character processing routines and the absolute value routine *abs*.

Specifically, the C preprocessor provides facilities for

- defining and removing macro definitions,
- inserting text from another file by physically including the contents of the specified file, and
- conditional inclusion of text.

C preprocessor facilities are not recognized by the C compiler. Consequently, the program, after having been processed by the C preprocessor, must be valid C code; otherwise, errors will be flagged by the C compiler.

1. MACRO DEFINITIONS

The C preprocessor macro definition facility provides the capability of associating an arbitrary string with an identifier. The preprocessor replaces every occurrence in the program of an identifier associated with a string with the string itself. Typically, the macro facility is used for defining symbolic constants, string replacement, and *in-line* functions. The first two items are implemented by using parameterless macros, and the last item by using parameterized macros.

It is important to note that the C preprocessor does not care about the nature of the string associated with an identifier; as far as it is concerned, the string can be arbitrary text. It is the programmer's responsibility to ensure that the string associated with the identifier will result in valid C code after the identifier is replaced by the string, and that it will not lead to a syntax error or a logical error. Syntax errors will be detected by the C compiler, but logical errors resulting from incorrect string definitions or incorrect use of string definitions, like other logical errors, must be discovered and diagnosed by the programmer.

By convention, upper-case letters are used for user-defined macro names (C implementations do not adhere to this convention for predefined macros). Although constant and string definitions are special cases of parameterized macros, they will be discussed separately (to reflect typical use).

1.1 CONSTANT DEFINITIONS

The C preprocessor macro facility is used for defining constants. This is because the C language does not have a constant definition mechanism (ANSI C will have such a mechanism).

Constants are defined using macro definitions of the form

```
#define constant-name  constant-expression
```

Some examples of constant definitions are

```
#define M 64
#define N 16
#define MAX 128
#define SIZE sizeof(int)
#define TOTAL (MAX*SIZE)
#define MASK 077
```

Here are some examples illustrating uses of the above definitions:

```
char a[M][N];
int *p;

p = (int *) malloc(TOTAL);

for (i=0; i<M; i++) ...

a = a & MASK;
```

Before the above code is compiled, it will be transformed by the C preprocessor to the code shown below by replacing the constant identifiers with their values:

```
char a[64][16];
int *p;

p = (int *) malloc((128*sizeof(int)));

for (i=0; i<64; i++) ...

a = a & 077;
```

Constant definitions make a program more readable and make it easier to modify. For example, suppose that a frequently used constant value is to be changed. If a constant identifier has been used, then this change will require only one modification (to the constant definition). If a constant identifier has not been used, but instead a literal value has been used directly, then every place where the literal has been used will require modification.

1.2 STRING DEFINITIONS

String definitions, which are similar to constant definitions, are used to give symbolic names to string constants and are also used as abbreviations for C source code. String definitions are of the form

#define *string-name* *sequence-of-characters*

Two example definitions are

```
#define FMT "x=%f, y=%f\n"
#define getchar() getc(stdin)
#define NXT_DATA_LN while(getchar() != '\n')
```

Constant *FMT* defines a string for use with a formatted output function as in the following *printf* function call:

```
printf(FMT, x, y);
```

The preprocessor will transform this function call to

```
printf("x=%f, y=%f\n", x, y);
```

The preprocessor transforms the macro call

```
getchar()
```

to the code

```
getc(stdin)
```

A semicolon was not given at the end of *getc(stdin)* in the definition of *getchar* because *getchar* can then look and be used like an ordinary function call. Here are two examples:

```
c = getchar();
while ((c == getchar()) != EOF) ...
```

The code associated with *NXT_DATA_LN* skips to the beginning of the next input line. Each use of

```
NXT_DATA_LN;
```

is replaced by the code

```
while(getchar() != '\n');
```

1.3 MACROS (IN-LINE FUNCTIONS)

Macros are essentially in-line functions. In the case of ordinary functions, a function call is translated into a jump to the code for the function body and at the end of the function a return jump to the statement following the function call is generated by the compiler. In case of macros, a macro call is textually replaced by the macro body after appropriately replacing the parameters with the corresponding arguments. Because of the textual replacement performed by the C preprocessor, no jumps to the beginning of the macro body and back from the end of the macro body are necessary.

Macros can be faster than functions; they should be used

- especially when implementing very small routines that are called from many places in the program, and

- when implementing a routine which is called from a small number of places in the program but which is called frequently during program execution.

The use of macros speeds up program execution due to the absence of jumps and due to the absence of the run-time copying of argument values to parameters. In case of very small macros or macros that are called only from a few places in the program, the size of the object file may also decrease. In other cases, the program size may actually increase.

Besides textual replacement of the macro calls by the corresponding macro bodies, there are other important differences between macros and functions. For example, macro names, unlike function names, cannot be passed as function arguments and side effects in macro arguments can lead to unexpected results (this is discussed later).

In a parameterized macro definition, the parameter names are specified along with the macro name and the macro body:

#define *macro-name* $(p_1, p_2, \ldots, p_n)$ *macro-body*

p_i are the macro parameters.

A macro call has the form

macro-name $(a_1, a_2, \ldots, a_n)$

where a_i are the macro arguments. This macro call will be replaced by the corresponding macro body, but only after each occurrence of the parameter p_i in the macro body has been replaced by the corresponding argument a_i.

Let us now look at some examples of parameterized macros. Here are some examples taken from the standard C header files such as *stdio.h* and *ctype.h*:

```
#define putchar(c)  putc(c,stdout)
#define rewind(fp)  fseek(fp,0L,0)

#define toupper(c)  (islower(c)?((c)-('a'-'A')):(c))
#define tolower(c)  (isupper(c)?((c)+('a'-'A')):(c))

#define abs(a)  ((a)<0 ? -(a):(a))
#define max(a,b)  ((a)>(b)?(a):(b))
#define min(a,b)  ((a)<(b)?(a):(b))
```

One interesting question to ask is why are there so many parentheses in the definitions of the macros *toupper*, *tolower*, *abs*, *max*, and *min*. The answer is safety and that is the focus of the next section.

To illustrate preprocessor expansion of parameterized macro calls, consider the call

```
max(x,y)
```

This call will be replaced by the expression

```
((x)>(y)?(x):(y))
```

Similarly the nested calls

```
max(x,max(y,z))
```

will be replaced by the expression

```
((x)>(((y)>(z)?(y):(z)))?(x):(((y)>(z)?(y):(z))))
```

Here are some examples of user-defined macro definitions:

```
#define SQR(x)  ((x)*(x))
#define PRINTI(x)  printf("x = %d\n", x)
```

PRINTI simplifies the printing of an integer variable's name along with its value. For example, the name of an integer variable *a* and its value can be printed as

```
PRINTI(a);
```

This call is replaced in the C source code by the body of *PRINTI* but after parameter *x* has been replaced by the argument *a*:

```
printf("a = %d\n", a);
```

1.4 SAFETY & GOOD PROGRAMMING PRACTICE

As in the case of functions, arbitrary expressions (which are arbitrary character sequences as far as the C preprocessor is concerned) can be given as arguments in a macro call. In the case of a function, the expression is evaluated and the result is the value assigned to the corresponding parameter. However, in the case of macros, each parameter is textually replaced at compile time by the corresponding unevaluated argument. Consequently, programmers should be careful when calling macros with arbitrary expressions. For example, parameter references in the macro body should be enclosed in parentheses.

As an illustration of the hazards that can be encountered if macro parameters are not enclosed in parentheses, consider the definition of the macro *SQR* which was given earlier:

```
#define SQR(x) ((x)*(x))
```

At a first glance, it appears that each of the three pairs of parentheses is superfluous. As it turns out, each pair of parentheses is essential. Suppose, for example, that we had not used these parentheses and we had instead defined *SQR* as

```
#define SQR(x) x*x
```

As long as *SQR* is called with simple variables and with adjacent operators having a lower precedence than ∗ there is no problem. The C preprocessor replaces the call

```
SQR(a)
```

by the text

```
a*a
```

which is what we want. Problems arise when *SQR* is called with arguments that are expressions. For example, the call

```
SQR(a+1)
```

will be expanded by the preprocessor into the expression

```
a+1*a+1
```

which is equivalent to the expression *2a+1* and not to the expected expression *(a+1)∗(a+1)*. This problem can be avoided by enclosing each occurrence of every macro parameter in the macro body within parentheses. If we do this, then the revised definition of *SQR* will look like

```
#define SQR(x) (x)*(x)
```

Now the call *SQR(a+1)* will be expanded to

```
(a+1)*(a+1)
```

which is what we want.

Enclosing each parameter within parentheses does not remove all potential problem situations. Consider the following expression

```
b/SQR(a)
```

in which we want to divide b by the square of a. Unfortunately, *SQR* will not work correctly and the value of the above expression will be just b. This is because the C preprocessor will expand the above call to

```
b/a*a
```

which is equivalent to the expression

```
(b/a)*a
```

This problem can be avoided by putting the whole macro body within parentheses, which leads us to the original definition of *SQR*:

```
#define SQR(x) ((x)*(x))
```

Finally, there is one more problem that can lead to errors when using macros: macro arguments with side effects. An expression with side effects is one that, when evaluated, causes a change in the value of a variable. Examples of expressions with side effects are expressions containing the assignment, the increment and the decrement operators. Giving an expression with side effects as a macro argument can cause problems if the corresponding parameter occurs more than once in the macro body. Each instance of the parameter in the macro body is replaced by the unevaluated expression argument. Consequently, each time the expression is evaluated, side effects will occur, once for each occurrence of the parameter in the macro body.

As an example, consider the macro call

```
SQR(a++)
```

which we expect to return a^2 and to increment a by 1. Unfortunately, this will not happen because the above call will be replaced by the expression

```
((a++)*(a++))
```

which, depending upon the compiler, will either evaluate to a^2 or a^2+1. In both cases, a will be incremented *twice* by 1.

Therefore, it is good programming practice to

- enclose all instances of a macro parameter in the macro body within parentheses,

- enclose the macro body in parentheses, and
- avoid calling macros with expressions that have side effects.

1.5 REMOVING (ERASING) MACRO DEFINITIONS

Some C preprocessors allow an existing macro to be redefined, but others will flag a macro redefinition as an error or, at the very least, issue a warning. To be on the safe side and for the program to be portable, old macro definitions should be removed explicitly before giving new macro definitions with the same name.

Macro definitions are removed using the *#undef* instruction which has the form

```
#undef name
```

Note that conditional compilation instructions (to be discussed later) can be used to determine whether or not a macro has been defined and then generate code based on this information.

2. SETS: PARAMETERIZED MACROS EXAMPLE

A set is a collection of objects no two of which are alike. Set operations include adding an element to and deleting an element from a set, checking set membership, taking the union, intersection and difference of two sets, iterating through all the elements of a set, determining the size of a set, and so forth.

One strategy for implementing a set is to use one word of memory for recording the elements present in the set. Each element of the set is assigned one of the bits: a zero bit value (bit off) indicates that the element is not in the set while a one bit value (bit on) indicates presence of the element in the set. This implementation is very simple and straightforward, but it does have one limitation: the maximum set size is limited to the number of bits in the word.

We will now define operations for manipulating a set of integers (from 0 to *MAXSETSIZE*-1); these operations will be defined as macros because they are very small, and the overhead of using functions will be significantly more than the cost of the actual set operations. Also, it will not be straightforward to define a function equivalent of the *foreach* loop for iterating through each element of the set.

Here is the header file for defining and manipulating set variables (stored in file *set.h*):

```
#define SET unsigned long
#define MAXSETSIZE (sizeof(SET)*8)

#define in(i, s) ((s) & (((SET) 1) << (i)))
#define add(i, s) ((s) | (((SET) 1) << (i)))
#define remove(i, s) ((s) & ~(((SET) 1) << (i)))
#define union(s, t) ((s) | (t))
#define intersection(s, t) ((s) & (t))
#define difference(s, t) ((s) & ~(t))
#define foreach(j, s) for(j=0;j<MAXSETSIZE;j++)\
                          if (in(j, (s)))
```

A set is represented using the largest unsigned integer allowed, that is, by using an *unsigned long* value (older C compilers may not allow unsigned long integers; check your compiler reference manual). In general, only unsigned integers should be used for bit manipulation because right shifting an unsigned word causes zero to be filled in the leftmost bit, while right shifting a signed word causes the sign bit to be propagated.

Checking to see whether or not an element is present in a set (operation *in*) is done by constructing a word with just the bit corresponding to the element having the value one and then performing a *bitwise and* with the set. If the element in question is present in the set, then the result of the *bitwise and* will be non-zero; otherwise, it will be zero. Element addition (operation *add*) is similar to set membership checking except that a *bitwise or* operation is performed instead of the *bitwise and*. Implementations of the other operations, i.e., *remove*, *union*, *intersection*, and *difference* are similarly straightforward and are therefore not explained here.

The *foreach* loop is a customized loop for iterating over all the elements of a set. It is not possible to write such a customized loop without macros (of course, one can always write the code in the definition of *foreach* directly in the program text). Notice the use of the backslash to continue the definition of *foreach* on to a new line.

Here are some examples illustrating use of the above macros:

```
SET s = 0, t = 0, z;
int i;

s = add(1,s);
s = add(2,s);
s = add(30,s); /*MAXSETSIZE == 32*/
s = remove(2, s);
z=intersection(s,t);

foreach(i, z) printf("%d ", i);
```

3. FILE INCLUSION

Typically, C program declarations that are used in several source files are kept in a separate file called a *header* file. The contents of this header file are then physically included in the files needing the declarations by using the C preprocessor *#include* instruction. Pascal does not have a file inclusion capability, although some Pascal compilers do provide such a facility. The *#include* instruction has two forms:

```
#include "fname"
#include <fname>
```

fname is the name of the file to be included (*fname* can also contain path information). The *#include* instruction can be nested, i.e., the included file can itself contain *#include* instructions. The maximum level of nesting is implementation dependent.

The only difference between the two forms of the *#include* instruction is that the first form (with the file name in quotes) looks for the specified file in the current directory before searching other implementation- or user-specified directories. (As a compile-time option, most C compilers allow the user to specify additional directories that are to be searched for the file to be included.) The second form of the *#include* instruction (with the file name in angle brackets) does not look for the file in the current directory.

The first form of the *#include* instruction (with the file name in quotes) is normally used for including user files and the second (with the file name in angle brackets) is used for including standard library files.

A path name, that is, a file name with directory information, can be given instead of a simple file name. On the MS-DOS system, backslashes are used to separate components of the path name while on UNIX systems slashes are used. Many MS-DOS system C compilers will accept both slashes and backslashes in the path name. For example, you can specify the path name as

```
/simulation/debug.h
```

or as

```
\simulation\debug.h
```

Although the *#include* instruction is typically used to include header files, any file, including C source files, can be included with it.

4. CONDITIONAL COMPILATION

Conditional compilation can be used to specify default macro definitions, to generate different versions of the same program and to avoid multiple file inclusions. The C preprocessor allows conditional compilation to be based on the value of a constant expression and whether or not a symbol has been defined.

4.1 CONDITIONAL COMPILATION BASED ON THE VALUE OF CONSTANT EXPRESSIONS

The *#if* instruction is used for conditionally compiling C code based on the value of a constant expression. This instruction has the forms

```
#if  constant-expression
       true-alternative-text
#endif
```

```
#if  constant-expression
       true-alternative-text
#else
       false-alternative-text
#endif
```

Like C, the preprocessor treats a non-zero value as true and a zero value as false. The text in each alternative can be an arbitrary sequence of characters including preprocessor instructions. Remember that the preprocessor does not understand C. It only understands lines beginning with the character #; to the C preprocessor, every thing else is just a sequence of characters.

4.2 CONDITIONAL COMPILATION BASED ON SYMBOL DEFINITION

The *#ifdef* and *#ifndef* instructions are used for conditionally compiling code depending upon whether or not the specified symbol has been defined. (Note that the specific string associated with the symbol is inconsequential.) The *#ifdef* instruction has the forms

```
#ifdef  symbol
         true-alternative-text
#endif
```

```
#ifdef  symbol
         true-alternative-text
#else
         false-alternative-text
#endif
```

The *#ifndef* instruction is similar to the *#ifdef* instruction, but it does the reverse. Instead of checking to see if a symbol has been defined, it checks to see if the symbol has *not* been defined.

The *#ifdef* and *#ifndef* instructions can be used to provide default constant (or default macro) definitions. For example, if an array size has not been explicitly specified, then a default size can be used:

```
#ifndef MAX_SIZE
#define MAX_SIZE 128
#endif
```

If identifier *MAX_SIZE* has defined before the above instructions are encountered, then it will not be given a new value; otherwise, it will be defined to have the value 128.

As another example of conditional compilation, suppose you are writing a C program that contains machine-dependent code for the IBM PC, Apple[TM], and Rainbow[TM] computers. When compiling code for a specific computer, only code for this particular computer is to be compiled. Here is how code that is to be conditionally compiled can be written:

```
#ifdef IBMPC
        code for the IBM PC computer
#endif
#ifdef APPLE
        code for the Apple computer
#endif
#ifdef RAINBOW
        code for the Rainbow computer
#endif
```

Now suppose you want to compile the program for the IBM PC. Then you must in an appropriate header file, which is to be included by all functions containing machine-dependent code, define the symbol IBMPC:

```
#define IBMPC 1
```

When compiling code for the Apple or the Rainbow computers, just replace this definition by a definition of the identifiers APPLE or RAINBOW, as appropriate.

4.3 PREDEFINED IDENTIFIERS FOR CONDITIONAL COMPILATION

Many C compilers predefine some identifiers for the convenience of the programmer to facilitate conditional compilation. Typically, the predefined symbols specify the computer and the operating system on which the program is being compiled. For instance, on the VAX[TM] computer, the C compiler will automatically define the symbol *vax*.

5. AVOIDING MULTIPLE FILE INCLUSIONS

Conditional compilation can also be invaluable when writing large programs consisting of many files that are written by several programmers. As an example, consider a function *test.c* that includes two header files, *sim.h* and *list.h*, as follows:

```
#include "sim.h"
#include "list.h"
```

Now suppose that the header file *sim.h* is modified to include the header file *list.h* because the declarations in *sim.h* have been changed and they now require the declarations in *list.h*. The two *#include* instructions shown above will cause *list.h* to be included twice in *test.c* leading to errors and warning messages which will be generated when *test.c* is compiled. The double inclusion of *list.h* can be avoided by using conditional compilation in conjunction with the following convention:

1. An identifier is associated with each header file for indicating whether or not the header file has been included.

2. Before including a file, check to determine whether or not the associated identifier is defined. If yes, then the file has already been included, and it should not be included again. Otherwise, include the file and define its associated identifier.

Continuing our example, suppose that identifiers *SIM* and *LIST* are associated with the header files *sim.h* and *list.h*. File *sim.h* includes file *list.h* as follows:

```
#ifndef LIST
#define LIST 1
#include "list.h"
#endif
```

Now the above paradigm will be used to include both the files *list.h* and *sim.h* in *test.c*:

```
#ifndef SIM
#define SIM 1
#include "sim.h"
#endif

#ifndef LIST
#define LIST 1
#include "list.h"
#endif
```

Use of the above paradigm ensures that file *list.h* will not be included twice in *test.c*.

6. EXERCISES

1. Write a macro *INT* that takes a single or double precision floating-point value x and returns the largest integer less than or equal to x.

2. Define *CLS* as an instruction to clear the screen (like the MS-DOS CLS instruction). It is to be used as

CLS;

3. List the pros and cons of using functions versus using macros.

4. Write a function version of the macro *PRINTI* (see Section 1.3) and then compare the macro and function versions.

5. What are the pros and cons of using enumeration types instead of the symbolic preprocessor constant definitions and vice versa.

6. How will you implement sets of size greater than the number of bits in an *unsigned long* type? Sketch the implementation of the set operations.

CHAPTER 8

LARGE EXAMPLES

Two relatively large examples will be given in this chapter to give the reader a better idea of how real programs are written using C. These programs illustrate a variety of C facilities and programming techniques such as

- program modularization,
- using external variables for inter-function communication,
- structures,
- reducing program size and enhancing readability with the preprocessor,
- type conversions,
- reading blocks of data from files and writing them to files,
- random file access,
- function *static* variables,
- using escape sequences to control the hardware, i.e., clear the screen and turn reverse video on/off, and
- a rare use of the *goto* statement.

The first example is a simplified version of a banking application and the second example is a simple document formatting program.

1. THE BANK TELLER PROGRAM

The problem is to write a program which will be used by a bank teller when interacting with a customer to update and query the bank database. For simplicity, we will assume that the bank is a very small one and that there is only one teller. This assumption ensures that only one program interacts with the database at any given time which frees us from worrying about problems that arise when multiple programs simultaneously query and update the same database records.

The bank teller can interact with the database in several ways. Teller interactions with the database are called *bank transactions*. A bank

155

transaction can have one of the following forms:

t
$t\ a_1$
$t\ a_1\ a_2$
$t\ a_1\ a_2\ a_3$

where t is a code specifying a bank transaction and a_1, a_2, and a_3 are transaction arguments. The description of the bank teller transactions along with their codes is given below. As appropriate, each transaction prints the requested information or it prints information about the bank account in question to show that the transaction was carried out successfully:

open new account (code "o")   Takes a client name as its argument, opens a new account, and returns the new account number.

close account (code "c")   Takes an account number as its argument and closes the specified account.

deposit money (code "d")   Takes two arguments—the account number and the amount to be deposited. It increments the balance in the specified account by the specified deposit.

withdraw money (code "w")   Takes two arguments—the account number and the amount to be withdrawn. A withdrawal is allowed only if there are sufficient funds in the specified account. If a withdrawal is allowed, then the account balance is reduced by the specified withdrawal amount.

transfer money (code "t")   Takes three arguments—the account numbers for the withdrawal and the deposit, and the amount to be transferred. Transfer of funds between the accounts is allowed only if the source account has sufficient funds.

balance (code "b")   Takes an account number as an argument and prints the balance in the account.

help (code "h")   Prints transaction codes and their arguments.

print (code "p") Prints information about all accounts (appropriate only for extremely small banks).

quit (code "q") Terminates the bank teller program.

The bank database is kept in a file named *bank.db* with the data being stored in the following format:

total number of accounts (including closed ones)
account$_1$
account$_2$
. . .
account$_n$

Each account has three fields: account number, customer name, and balance. Closed accounts will be indicated by a zero account number. One question to ask is why not physically remove the information about a closed account from the file. One important reason for not doing this is that banks like to keep information about closed accounts for any questions that may need to be answered at a later time. In practice, information about closed accounts is physically removed from bank databases after a specified time period. Another reason for not physically removing information is that physically deleting an account requires more work than just changing the account number to zero; specifically, all the accounts after the closed account must be shifted to close up the gap that arises because of the closed account.

The bank teller program that will be shown here is partitioned into several modules: the header file, the file containing the main program, and the files containing the functions implementing the bank transactions. Let us first look at the header file, *bnk.h*, which is included by all the other modules because it contains declarations needed by them:

```
#include <stdio.h>

#define LL 64
#define INTI (int) sizeof(int)
#define INTL (long) sizeof(int)
#define ACTI (int) sizeof(account)
#define ACTL (long) sizeof(account)
#define SUCCESS 1
#define FAILURE 0

#define NXT_DATA_LN while(getchar() != '\n')

typedef struct {
    int no;    /* == 0 means closed */
    char name[LL];
    double bal;
} account;

extern FILE *fp;
extern int n;

void openact(), help(), printact(), printdb();
int balance(), closeact(), deposit(),
    withdraw();
```

The interesting aspect of this header file is the use of the C preprocessor to define abbreviations representing C source code. For instance, the random file access functions, such as *fseek*, *fread* and *fwrite*, require that the record size argument should be of either the type *int* or the type *long* depending upon the function. However, the *sizeof* operator, which is used to compute the record size, returns *unsigned* values. Consequently, the cast operator must be used to convert the value returned by *sizeof* operator to the type required by the file access functions. Without the use of the preprocessor constant definitions—*INTI*, *INTL*, *ACTI*, and *ACTL*—calls to the file functions (which we shall see later) will be textually long and this may make the code hard to read in some cases.

Another example of code abbreviation is the symbol *NXT_DATA_LN* which is defined as a loop that skips to the beginning of the next line. Note the absence of the semicolon at the end of the loop. This means that every use of *NXT_DATA_LN* must be followed by a semicolon that will make each use of *NXT_DATA_LN* look like a C statement.

Structure type *account* specifies components for holding information associated with a single bank account. This makes it convenient to manipulate account information. For example, a single *account* variable can be used to store all the information associated with one account and giving this variable as an argument to a function provides the function with all the information about the account.

External variables *fp* and *n* are used for inter-function communication. Although parameters could also have been used, it is more convenient to use external variables for inter-function communication because the same variables are to be passed as arguments every time. This makes the function calls shorter and increases program efficiency (in this case by a small amount) by eliminating the need to copy the argument values to the corresponding parameters.

The two external variables, *fp*, and *n*, are used by most of the functions in the bank teller program. *fp* and *n* will be defined only in function *main* but their declarations will be included in all files that refer to them. Variable *fp* is initialized to the bank database file *bank.db*, and *n* is initialized to the total number of accounts (including closed ones). Because *main* contains the definitions of these variables, it is not necessary to include their declarations in *main* (provided they are used after their definitions are encountered). Nevertheless, their declarations are included in *main* as a side effect of including file *bnk.h* which, among other things, contains their declarations. Note that file *bnk.h* is included in *main* for the declarations of other variables that are needed by *main*. Redundant declarations are harmless provided they do not clash with each other or with the corresponding definitions.

The *main* program (stored in file *bnk.c*) consists essentially of one big *switch* statement. It reads the transaction code and the transaction arguments entered by the bank teller and then calls the appropriate function. Both external variables *fp* and *n* are defined and initialized in function *main*:

```
#include "bnk.h"

FILE *fp;
int n = 0;   /*number of accounts including*/
             /*deleted ones*/

main()
{
    char name[LL];
    int code, no, no2;
    double amt;

    puts("Good Morning!");
    if ((fp = fopen("bank.db", "r+"))==NULL) {
        puts("error, cannot open \"bank.db\"");
        exit(1);
    }
    fread((char *) &n, INTI, 1, fp);
    for (;;) {
        switch (code = getchar()) {
        case 'o':
            openact(gets(name));
            break;
        case 'c':
        case 'b':
            scanf("%d", &no);
            NXT_DATA_LN;
            if (code == 'c')
                closeact(no);
            else
                balance(no);
            break;
        case 'd':
        case 'w':
            scanf("%d%lf", &no, &amt);
            NXT_DATA_LN;
            if (code == 'd')
                deposit(no, amt);
            else
                withdraw(no, amt);
            break;
        case 't':
            scanf("%d%d%lf", &no, &no2, &amt);
            NXT_DATA_LN;
            if (withdraw(no, amt) == SUCCESS)
                deposit(no2, amt);
            break;
        case 'h':
            NXT_DATA_LN;
            help();
            break;
```

```
            case 'p':
                NXT_DATA_LN;
                printdb();
                break;
            case 'q':
                fclose(fp);
                exit(0);
            default:
                NXT_DATA_LN;
                puts("error, try again");
            }
        }
}
```

Function *main* opens the database file and eventually closes it when the bank teller quits by typing the transaction code "q". Other functions do not have to worry about opening and closing the database file.

Money transfer from one account to another is treated as a two-stage transaction: a successful withdrawal followed by a deposit. This allows functions used for withdrawing and depositing money to be used also for inter-account money transfer. This eliminates the need for writing a new function just for doing inter-account money transfer. Note that writing programs as a collection of small and appropriately parameterized functions encourages the reuse of existing software.

Notice the use of the backslash to include the double quote character in a string literal given as the argument in the *puts* function call:

```
puts("error, cannot open \"bank.db\"");
```

As mentioned earlier, preceding a character by a backslash either suppresses the special role of the character in the language (as in "\"") or gives the character some special meaning (as in "\n" which denotes the newline character).

Opening an account is a matter of rewinding the file (moving to the beginning of the file), writing the total number of accounts (one more than before), seeking (moving) to the end of the file, and writing a record for the new account. Here is function *openact* (stored in file *bnkopn.c*) which is used to open a new account:

```
#include "bnk.h"

void openact(name)
    char name[];
{
    account a;

    a.no = ++n;
    strcpy(a.name, name);
    a.bal = 0;

    rewind(fp);
    fwrite((char *) &n, INTI, 1, fp);
    fseek(fp, (long) (INTL+(n-1)*ACTL), 0);
            /*move to end of file*/
    fwrite((char *) &a, ACTI, 1, fp);
    printact(&a);
}
```

As mentioned earlier, an account is closed by simply setting the account number to 0. Here is the function *closeact* (stored in file *bnkclo.c*):

```
#include "bnk.h"

int closeact(no)
    int no;
{
    account a;

    if (no > n) {
        printf("error, act %d non existent\n",no);
        return FAILURE;
    }
    rewind(fp);
    fseek(fp, INTL+(no-1)*ACTL, 1);
    fread((char *) &a, ACTI, 1, fp);
    if (a.no == no) {
        printact(&a);
        if (a.bal == 0.0)
            printf("account closed\n");
        else {
            printf("account closed,
                    pay customer $%.2f\n", a.bal);
            a.bal = 0.0;
        }
        a.no = 0;
        fseek(fp, -ACTL, 1);
        fwrite((char *) &a, ACTI, 1, fp);
        return SUCCESS;
    }
    printf("error, act %d already closed\n", no);
    return FAILURE;
}
```

Function *deposit* is called when a client makes a deposit (stored in file *bnkdep.c*):

```
#include "bnk.h"

int deposit(no, amt)
    int no;
    double amt;
{
    account a;

    if (no > n) {
        printf("error, act %d non existent\n",no);
        return FAILURE;
    }
    if (amt < 0) {
        puts("error, deposit should be positive");
        return FAILURE;
    }
    rewind(fp);
    fseek(fp, INTL+(no-1)*ACTL, 1);
    fread((char *) &a, ACTI, 1, fp);
    if (a.no == no) {
        a.bal += amt;  /*note, no overflow check*/
        fseek(fp, -ACTL, 1);
        fwrite((char *) &a, ACTI, 1, fp);
        printact(&a);
        return SUCCESS;
    }
    printf("error, account %d is closed\n", no);
    return FAILURE;
}
```

Function *withdraw* (stored in file *bnkwit.c*) is called when a client wants to withdraw money:

```c
#include "bnk.h"

int withdraw(no, amt)
    int no;
    double amt;
{
    account a;

    if (no > n) {
        printf("error, act %d non existent\n",no);
        return FAILURE;
    }
    if (amt < 0) {
        puts("error, withdrawl should be positive");
        return FAILURE;
    }
    rewind(fp);
    fseek(fp, INTL+(no-1)*ACTL, 1);
    fread((char *) &a, ACTI, 1, fp);
    if (a.no == no) {
        if (a.bal - amt < 0) {
            puts("insuffient funds in account");
            printact(&a);
            return FAILURE;
        }
        a.bal -= amt;
        fseek(fp, -ACTL, 1);
        fwrite((char *) &a, ACTI, 1, fp);
        printact(&a);
        return SUCCESS;
    }
    printf("error, act %d is closed\n", no);
    return FAILURE;
}
```

Function *balance* (stored in file *bnkbal.c*) is used to print the account balance:

```
#include "bnk.h"

int balance(no)
    int no;
{
    account a;

    if (no > n) {
        printf("error, act %d non existent\n", no);
        return FAILURE;
    }
    rewind(fp);
    fseek(fp, INTL+(no-1)*ACTL, 1);
    fread((char *) &a, ACTI, 1, fp);
    if (a.no == no) {
        printact(&a); return SUCCESS;
    }
    printf("error, account %d is closed\n", no);
    return FAILURE;
}
```

Here is the *help* function (stored in file *bnkhlp.c*) which prints information about transaction codes and their arguments for the convenience of the bank teller:

```
#include "bnk.h"

void help()
{
    puts("\033[2J"); /*clear screen*/
    puts("\033[7mo\033[0mpen Firstname Lastname");
            /*\033[7m turns on reverse video */
            /*\033[0m turns off reverse video*/
    puts("\033[7mc\033[0mlose ActNo");
    puts("\033[7md\033[0meposit ActNo Amount");
    puts("\033[7mw\033[0mithdraw ActNo Amount");
    puts("\033[7mt\033[0mransfer From To Amount");
    puts("\033[7mb\033[0malance ActNo");
    puts("\033[7mh\033[0melp");
    puts("\033[7mq\033[0muit");
    puts("");
}
```

Note the use of escape sequences to clear the screen ("\033[2J") and to turn reverse video on ("\033[7m") and off ("\033[0m"). Escape sequences are not printed. Instead they just change the monitor display characteristics. If you are interested in more details about escape sequences, see the *IBM DOS Technical Reference Manual* [IBM83b] or a technical reference manual appropriate for your hardware.

The next two functions (stored in file *bnkprt.c*) are straightforward: *printact* prints an account record and *printdb* prints the whole database:

```
#include "bnk.h"

void printact(a)
    account *a;
{
    printf("act no = %d, name = %s,
                        balance = %.2f\n",
                        a->no, a->name, a->bal);
}

void printdb()
{
    int i;
    account a;

    rewind(fp);
    puts("\033[2J"); /*clear screen*/
    printf("Number of Accounts=%d\n", n);
    fseek(fp, INTL, 1);
    for (i=0; i<n; i++) {
        fread((char *) &a, ACTI, 1, fp);
        printact(&a);
    }
}
```

To produce an executable form of the bank teller program, the component modules must be compiled and linked together. (In case of the Lattice C compiler, the program must be linked with the math library because the print routines for floating point numbers are stored there.)

2. THE TEXT FORMATTER

The problem is to write a simple "batch-oriented" text formatter (in contrast to a "wysiwyg" formatter)* that takes a text document, interspersed with text formatting commands, and formats the document text as specified by the formatting commands. These commands begin with the character "@" in column one.

By default, the formatter operates in the *fill* and *justify* modes in which as many words as possible are fitted on a line. In the justify mode blanks are inserted between words, whenever necessary, to right justify the text. Note that blanks are not inserted before the first word or after the last word; otherwise, the text will not be left and right justified, respectively. Blanks are also not inserted before a punctuation mark, such as a comma, that immediately follows a word without a separating blank.

The fill mode can be turned off. In case of the no-fill or copy mode all input lines, except formatting commands, are copied from the input to the output without any formatting, until a formatting command specifying a change to the fill mode is encountered.

Here are the formatting commands that are to be implemented:

@*p*   Begin a new paragraph.

@*np*   Begin a new page.

@*nf*   Turn off fill mode, that is, switch to fill mode.

@*fi*   Restore fill mode.

The formatter program is partitioned into several modules each of which contains one function. These functions are listed below:

    main   Decision making function that gets tokens, assembles, and prints lines.

    justify   Function that justifies a line by filling blanks.

---

* When using a batch-oriented formatter, the formatting commands are interspersed with the document text. The formatted version of the document can be viewed only after the document is processed with the formatter. It is only then that you get to see the effects of the formatting commands. In contrast, with a "wysiwyg" (what-you-see-is-what-you-get) formatter, you see the formatted output as it is entered into the computer. The wysiwyg formatter interprets the formatting commands right away; it does not wait until after you have entered the whole document.

> *token* Function that returns the token type as the function result
> and the token itself in the function argument; tokens are
> items such as a space, a word or a format specifier.
>
> *printline* Print line function.
>
> *error* Function for printing an error message.

For this simple formatter, it was convenient to think of a word as a sequence
of text characters (excluding those making up the formatting commands)
terminated by a blank, a newline, or a formatting command. Consequently,
punctuation marks immediately following a word are considered to be part of
the word itself ensuring that they will not be separated from the word by
being put on the next line or by blanks inserted in the line to right justify it.

Here is the file *fmt.h* which contains declarations used by the various
modules:

```
#include <stdio.h>

    /*token type*/
#define SPACE   0
#define NOFILL  1
#define FILL    2
#define NEWPAGE 3
#define NL      4
#define PARA    5
#define WORD    6

#define LL 80
#define WL 80

extern char word[][WL];
    /*word[i] contains word i of current line*/
    /*only first dimension can be unspecified*/
extern int spaces[];
    /*spaces[i]: word[i] begins spaces[i]    */
    /*after word[i-1]*/
extern int w,  /*w=no words in line*/
         ll; /*ll is line length */

void printline(), justify(), error();
int token();
```

Instead of using *#define* instructions for specifying the token types, a single
enumeration type could also have been used. Nevertheless, an enumeration
type was not used because, as mentioned before, not all compilers implement
the enumeration type. Use of enumeration types can therefore be
detrimental to program portability.

The formatter starts by processing text in the fill and justify modes. It gets tokens, the pieces into which the document to be formatted is disassembled, by calling function *token*. In the fill mode, the formatter assembles a line, storing the words in the two-dimensional array *word*. Spaces between words are noted in array *spaces*. No spaces are printed before the first word or after the last word. When no more words can be put in the current line, the line is right justified (by calling function *justify*) and then printed (by calling function *printline*).

Upon encountering a new paragraph, new page, or change to no-fill mode formatting command, the output line currently being assembled is printed without right justification.

In the (no-fill) copy mode, the formatter copies the input read by it directly to the output obeying formatting commands, until it encounters the command restoring the fill mode of operation.

We will now show you the *main* function (stored in file *fmt.c*) which is the heart of the formatter program:

```
#include "fmt.h"

char word[LL][WL];
int spaces[LL];
int w = 0, ll = 60;

/*line length (<LL) can be specified on the*/
/*command line*/

main(argc, argv)
   int argc; char *argv[];
{
   char a[WL];
   int type, n = 0, nofill = 0, sp = 0, odd =0;
      /*n == current line length*/
      /*sp == spaces between words*/

   if (argc == 2) sscanf(argv[1], "%d", &ll);
   while ((type = token(a)) != EOF) {
     switch (type) {
       case NOFILL:
         nofill = 1; printline();
         w = n = sp = 0;
         if (token(a) != NL)
            error("newline expected");
         continue;
       case FILL:
         nofill = 0;
         if (token(a) != NL)
            error("newline expected");
```

```
            continue;
        case NEWPAGE:
        case PARA:
          printline();
          putchar(type == PARA ? '\n' : '\f');
          w = n = sp = 0;
          if (token(a) != NL)
              error("newline expected");
          continue;
        default:
          ;
    }
    if (nofill) {printf("%s", a); continue;}
nextline:
    if (n + strlen(a) <= ll) {
        if (type == NL || type == SPACE) {
          if (w != 0) {n++; sp++;}
              /*no spaces before first word*/
        }
        else {
          spaces[w] = sp; sp = 0;
          strcpy(word[w++], a); n += strlen(a);
        }
    }
    else {
        justify(n-sp, odd = !odd);
          /*n-sp == total # of characters in line*/
          /*minus trailing spaces*/
        printline(); w = n = sp = 0;
        goto nextline;
    }
  }
  if (w != 0)  /*flush out the last few words*/
    printline();
}
```

Notice the use of the *goto* statement. After determining that the next token will not fit on the line currently being assembled, the line is printed, and the token is then inserted in the next line. The *goto* statement is used to jump back to the code for inserting a token into a line. There is no need to get a new token because the last token still has to be processed (we will get a new token if we just continue with the next iteration of the loop). In general, the use of *goto* statements can be detrimental to program readability and understandability. Although *goto* statements can always be avoided, sometimes as in this example, their use is convenient (and appropriate). We could have avoided the use of the *goto* by using a "flag" variable.

The absence of any statements in the *NEWPAGE* alternative effectively means that both *NEWPAGE* and *PARA* are labels for the same set of statements. Note that in the *NEWPAGE* and *PARA* alternative the *continue* statement is used instead of the *break* statement to terminate execution of the *switch* statement. The *continue* statement initiates the next iteration of the surrounding loop which ensures that control does not flow on to the next alternative (*default* alternative in this case).

Function *justify* right justifies a line by inserting blanks between the words. For odd lines it starts inserting blanks from the left side of the line and for even lines it starts from the right side. Alternating the direction from which the blanks are inserted avoids "holes" from appearing in the text. Here is the function *justify* (stored in file *fmtjst.c*):

```
#include "fmt.h"

void justify(nch, odd)
  int nch, odd;
      /*nch:no of char in line    */
      /*odd==1: odd numbered line */
      /*odd==0: even numbered line*/
{
  int i, nblnk = 11 - nch;

  i = odd ? 1 : w-1;
  while (nblnk >0) {
    spaces[i]++; nblnk--;
    if (odd)
      i = i < w-1 ? i+1 : 1;
    else
      i = i > 1 ? i-1 : w-1;
  }
}
```

Function *printline* (stored in file *fmtprtl.h*) prints the words stored in the two-dimensional array *word*, inserting spaces between the words according to the values of the elements in array *spaces*:

```
#include "fmt.h"

void printline()
{
  int j, k;
  for (j=0; j<w; j++) {
    for (k=0; k < spaces[j]; k++)
      putchar(' ');
    printf("%s", word[j]);
  }
  putchar('\n');
}
```

The error printing function *error* (stored in file *fmterr.c*) is straightforward:

```
#include "fmt.h"

void error(msg)
  char *msg;
{
  printf("Error: %s\n", msg);
  exit(1);
}
```

Now it is time to take a look at function *token* that disassembles the input text into tokens. This function returns the token type as the function result, and it stores the token text in the address pointed to by the function parameter *s*. Character "@" is treated specially only if it begins in column one; in this case it must begin a valid formatter command. Here is the function *token* (stored in file *fmttkn.c*):

```
#include <ctype.h>
#include "fmt.h"

int token(s)
  char *s;  /*string for holding token*/
{
  int c, i;
  static int col = 0;

  while ((c = getchar()) != EOF) {
    col++;
    if (c == ' ') {
        s[0] = c; s[1] = '\0';
        return SPACE;
    }
    else if (c == '\n') {
        s[0] = c; s[1] = '\0'; col = 0;
        return NL;
    }
    else if (c == '@' && col == 1) {
        s[0] = c; s[2] = '\0';
        switch(s[1] = getchar()) {
          case 'p':
            return PARA;
          case 'n':
          case 'f':
            s[2] = getchar(); s[3] = '\0';
            if (strcmp(s, "@nf") == 0)
                return NOFILL;
            else if (strcmp(s, "@fi") == 0)
                return FILL;
            else if (strcmp(s, "@np") == 0)
                return NEWPAGE;
          default:
            fprintf(stderr,
                "token: illegal @ cmd: %s\n",s);
            exit(1);
        }
    }
    else {
        s[0] = c; i = 1;
        while(!isspace(c=getchar())) s[i++] = c;
        s[i] = '\0';
        if (c != EOF) ungetc(c, stdin);
        return WORD;
    }
  }
  return EOF;
}
```

Variable *col* is defined with the storage class *static* so that it retains its value across multiple calls to function *token*. *col* could also have been declared as an external variable in which case it would also retain its value across function calls. However, declaring *col* as an external variable would make it visible to other functions disregarding the fact that they may have no need to access *col*. Therefore, declaring *col* as an external variable increases the chances of some function erroneously accessing or updating it.

Note that strings are compared using the library function *strcmp*. Unlike the equality operator in Pascal, the C equality operator = = cannot be used to compare strings because, as mentioned before, strings are not a built-in data type in C. The function call *strcmp(s, t)* returns a negative, zero or positive value, depending upon whether string *s* is lexicographically less than, identical to, or greater than string *t*. Comparing two strings using the equality operator is not flagged as an error by the C compiler because C interprets it as a comparison of the pointers that refer to the beginning of the two strings. Of course, it is possible that you may sometimes fortuitously get the right result.

3. EXERCISES

1. How can you make the bank teller's program more robust? That is, catch more errors and give better diagnostics?

2. Almost all large computer operating systems, including some PC operating systems, allow multiple users to simultaneously use the computer. Can you give scenarios illustrating problems that could occur if two bank tellers try to simultaneously open a new account or update an existing account?

3. What facilities are needed to prevent two bank tellers from simultaneously updating the same bank account or preventing one bank teller from updating the account while the other is querying it?

4. What additional functionality can you add to the bank teller program?

5. Modify function *justify* so that it justifies a line by always inserting blanks starting from the same direction, that is, there should be no difference in justifying odd or even numbered lines. Compare the formatted output using the modified *justify* with the formatted output produced using the original definition of *justify*.

6. The formatting program does not paginate. To be specific, it just prints its output one line after another ignoring page boundaries. Therefore, it does not leave space for the customary top and bottom margins on a page. Modify the formatting program so that it leaves a few blank lines both at the top and bottom of each page.

7. Extend the formatting program with additional formatting commands such as center the next line, change indentation, stop and resume right justification, change the line length, and specify alternative page sizes.

APPENDIX 1

C LIBRARY FUNCTIONS

C is a small and relatively simple language; for example, its reference manual is about 40 book size pages [Kern78]. This is in contrast to languages, such as PL/I and the Ada language, whose size and complexity are reflected by their rather large reference manuals. C adopts the philosophy that only the important and essential facilities will be in the language itself. Other facilities will be provided as components of standard libraries that will come with each C compiler. Therefore, many facilities that are part of languages such as FORTRAN, PL/I and Pascal are provided as library routines (macros and functions) in C. We shall discuss the following categories of standard library routines:

1. Storage allocation and deallocation.

2. Character processing.

3. String processing.

4. Input/output.

5. System interaction.

6. Math.

C compilers usually provide header files that contain declarations of the library functions and items related to the functions. Consequently, instead of writing the function declarations explicitly, C programmers typically include the appropriate header files by using the C preprocessor *#include* instruction.

When describing a C library function, we will first give its specification and then discuss its functionality. The specification of a function consists of three parts:

1. Declarations necessary for using the function. In some cases these declarations can be omitted, but in general, their presence is necessary for proper use of the functions.

2. The first line of the function definition.

3.   One or more lines of parameter declarations.

For ease of reference, functions within each of the categories mentioned above will be listed in alphabetical order.

1.   STORAGE ALLOCATION

Many C compilers do not provide a header file that contains the declarations of the storage allocation and deallocation functions. The Lattice C compiler is an exception; it provides a header file, *stdlib.h*, that contains the declarations of these functions.

1.1   CALLOC: ALLOCATE & CLEAR MEMORY (also see MALLOC)

```
#include <stdlib.h>
char *calloc(nelem, elemsize)
    unsigned nelem, elemsize;
```

Allocates a block of memory of size *nelem*elemsize* bytes with all the bits of the allocated storage set to zero. If storage can be allocated, *calloc* returns a (character) pointer to the beginning of the allocated block of storage; otherwise, it returns the null pointer *NULL*. Typically, *elemsize* is specified using the *sizeof* operator and the character pointer returned as the result is cast to a pointer to the desired element type.

1.2   MALLOC: ALLOCATE MEMORY (also see CALLOC)

```
#include <stdlib.h>
char *malloc(n)
    unsigned n;
```

Allocates a block of memory of size *n* bytes. If successful, *malloc* returns a (character) pointer to the beginning of this block; otherwise, it returns the null pointer *NULL*. Typically, the character pointer returned as the result is cast to a pointer to the desired element type.

1.3   FREE: FREE MEMORY

```
#include <stdlib.h>
int free(ptr)
    char *ptr;
```

Frees (deallocates) a previously allocated memory block pointed to by *ptr*. This memory block should not have been previously deallocated and the value of *ptr* must be one that was previously returned by one of the memory allocation functions. A freed memory block should not be reused by the programmer because the storage allocation functions may have reallocated this storage already.

1.4 REALLOC: REALLOCATE MEMORY

```
#include <stdlib.h>
char *realloc(ptr, n)
    char *ptr;
    unsigned n;
```

Takes a pointer *ptr* to a previously allocated memory block and changes the size of the memory block to *n* while preserving its contents. If necessary, the contents of the current block are copied to a new memory block of the requested size. If *n* is less than the current block size, then only the contents of the first *n* bytes of the old block are preserved. The pointer returned by *realloc* can be

1. equal to *ptr* indicating that the current block size was simply increased,

2. different from *ptr* indicating that a new memory block was allocated, the contents of the old block copied to the new block, and the block pointed to by the original value of *ptr* deallocated, or

3. the null pointer indicating that it was not possible to do the requested reallocation.

Typically, the character pointer returned as the result is cast to a pointer to the desired element type.

2. CHARACTER MANIPULATION

Character manipulation routines are implemented either as macros or as functions. Some compilers provide both macro and function versions. As discussed in Chapter 7, macros can speed up program execution time, but the storage required for the program may increase. Functions may sometimes be preferred to macros because, unlike macros, they can be passed as arguments in function calls. Also, macros can lead to unexpected results if they are invoked with arguments that have side effects.

The Lattice C compiler provides both macro and function versions of the character processing routines. To use the macro versions of these routines, include the header file *ctype.h*. This file contains the definitions of the macro versions of the character processing routines.

Character processing routines are of two kinds: *classification* and *conversion*. The classification routines, which begin with the prefix *is*, are used for determining the type of a character, e.g., *isalpha*. The conversion functions convert a lower-case character to upper case and vice versa, and any character to its ASCII representation. A summary of the character processing routines commonly provided by C compilers is given below.

2.1 ISALNUM: ALPHANUMERIC TEST

```
#include <ctype.h>
int isalnum(c)
    char c;
```

Returns a non-zero value if *c* is an alphanumeric character; otherwise, zero.

2.2 ISALPHA: ALPHABETIC TEST

```
#include <ctype.h>
int isalpha(c)
    char c;
```

Returns a non-zero value if *c* is an alphabetic character; otherwise, zero.

2.3 ISASCII: ASCII TEST

```
#include <ctype.h>
int isascii(c)
    char c;
```

Returns a non-zero value if *c* is an ASCII character; otherwise, zero.

2.4 ISCNTRL: CONTROL CHARACTER TEST

```
#include <ctype.h>
int iscntrl(c)
    char c;
```

Returns a non-zero value if *c* is a control character; otherwise, zero.

2.5 ISCSYM: C IDENTIFIER CHARACTER TEST

```
#include <ctype.h>
int iscsym(c)
    char c;
```

Returns a non-zero value if *c* is a character that can be used to construct a C identifier; otherwise, zero.

2.6 ISCSYMF: C IDENTIFIER FIRST CHARACTER TEST

```
#include <ctype.h>
int iscsymf(c)
    char c;
```

Returns a non-zero value if *c* is a character that can be the first character of a C identifier; otherwise, zero.

2.7 ISDIGIT: DIGIT TEST

```
#include <ctype.h>
int isdigit(c)
    char c;
```

Returns a non-zero value if *c* is a digit; otherwise, zero.

2.8 ISGRAPH: GRAPHIC CHARACTER TEST

```
#include <ctype.h>
int isgraph(c)
    char c;
```

Returns a non-zero value if *c* is a graphic character (any printing character other than a space); otherwise, zero.

2.9 ISLOWER: LOWER-CASE CHARACTER TEST

```
#include <ctype.h>
int islower(c)
    char c;
```

Returns a non-zero value if *c* is a lower-case character; otherwise, zero.

2.10 ISPRINT: PRINTING CHARACTER TEST

```
#include <ctype.h>
int isprint(c)
    char c;
```

Returns a non-zero value if *c* is a printing character; otherwise, zero.

2.11 ISPUNCT: PUNCTUATION TEST

```
#include <ctype.h>
int ispunct(c)
    char c;
```

Returns a non-zero value if *c* is a space or a punctuation character; otherwise, zero.

2.12 ISSPACE: WHITE SPACE CHARACTER TEST

```
#include <ctype.h>
int isspace(c)
    char c;
```

Returns a non-zero value if *c* is a white space character, that is, if *c* is a horizontal or a vertical tab, or a formfeed, a newline, a carriage return or a space character; otherwise, zero.

2.13 ISUPPER: UPPER CHARACTER TEST

```
#include <ctype.h>
int isupper(c)
    char c;
```

Returns a non-zero value if *c* is an upper-case character; otherwise, zero.

2.14 ISXDIGIT: HEXADECIMAL DIGIT TEST

```
#include <ctype.h>
int isxdigit(c)
    char c;
```

Returns a non-zero value if *c* is a hexadecimal digit; otherwise, zero.

2.15 TOASCII: CONVERT TO ASCII

```
#include <ctype.h>
int toascii(c)
    char c;
```

Returns the ASCII version of character *c* by discarding all but the 7 low bits of *c*.

2.16 TOLOWER: CONVERT TO LOWER CASE

```
#include <ctype.h>
int tolower(c)
    char c;
```

Returns the lower-case version of *c* if *c* is an upper-case letter; otherwise, *c*.

2.17 TOUPPER: CONVERT TO UPPER CASE

```
#include <ctype.h>
int toupper(c)
    char c;
```

Returns the upper-case version of *c* if *c* is a lower-case letter; otherwise, *c*.

3. STRING PROCESSING

All string processing routines assume that the string is terminated by the *null* character. String routines can be classified into the following types: concatenation, copy, comparison, length, and search.

3.1 STRCAT: CONCATENATE STRINGS

```
#include <string.h>
char *strcat(d, s)
    char *d, *s;
```

Concatenate (append) a copy of the source string *s* to the end of the destination string *d*. The terminating null character in *d* is overwritten with characters from *s* and a new terminating null character is added after the appended characters.

Note that for the proper operation of *strcat* the storage allocated for string *d* should be large enough to accommodate the additional characters being copied from *s*, and strings *d* and *s* should not overlap.

3.2 STRCHR: SEARCH FOR THE FIRST OCCURRENCE OF A CHARACTER

```
#include <string.h>
char *strchr(s, c)
    char *s, c;
```

If *c* is in string *s*, then *strchr* returns a pointer to the first occurrence of *c*; otherwise, it returns the null pointer *NULL*. The null character terminating *s* is also considered to be in *s*.

3.3 STRCMP: COMPARE TWO STRINGS

```
#include <string.h>
int strcmp(a, b)
    char *a, *b;
```

Returns a negative, a zero, or a positive integer value depending upon whether the string *a* is lexicographically less than, equal to, or greater than the string *b* (the ASCII collating sequence is used for the comparison).

3.4 STRICMP: COMPARE TWO STRINGS IGNORING CASE DIFFERENCES

```
#include <string.h>
int stricmp(a, b)
    char *a, *b;
```

Same as *strcmp* except that case differences between the corresponding letters in the argument strings *a* and *b* are ignored.

3.5 STRCPY: COPY STRING

```
#include <string.h>
char *strcpy(d, s)
    char *d, *s;
```

Copies source string *s* to destination string *d*, including the terminating null character, and returns the pointer to the beginning of *d* (the value passed to *strcpy*).

Note that for the proper operation of *strcpy*, the length of string *d* should be greater than or equal to that of string *s*, and strings *d* and *s* should not overlap.

3.6 STRCSPN: MEASURE SPAN (COUNT NUMBER) OF CHARACTERS NOT IN SET

```
#include <string.h>
int strcspn(a, b)
    char *a, *b;
```

Returns the number of leading characters of string *a* that are not in the character set specified by string *b*.

3.7 STRLEN: STRING LENGTH

```
#include <string.h>
int strlen(s)
    char *s;
```

Returns the length of string *s*.

3.8 STRNCAT: CONCATENATE *n* CHARACTERS

```
#include <string.h>
char *strncat(d, s, n)
    char *d, *s;
    int n;
```

Concatenate (append) the first *n* characters of source string *s* to the end of destination string *d*. The terminating null character in string *d* is overwritten with characters from *s* and a new terminating null character appended at the end of the appended characters. If *n* is greater than the length of *s*, then *strncat(d, s, n)* is equivalent to *strcat(d, s)*.

Note that for the proper operation of *strncat*, the storage allocated for string *s* should be large enough to accommodate the additional *n* characters, and strings *d* and *s* should not overlap.

3.9 STRNCMP: COMPARE UP TO *n* CHARACTERS OF TWO STRINGS

```
#include <string.h>
int strncmp(a, b, n)
    char *a, *b;
    int n;
```

Same as *strcmp* except that at most the first *n* characters of the two strings are compared.

3.10 STRNCPY: COPY *n* CHARACTERS OF STRING

```
#include <string.h>
char *strncpy(d, s, n)
    char *d, *s;
    int n;
```

Copies *n* characters of the source string *s* to the destination string *d* and returns a pointer to the beginning of *d* (the value passed to *strncpy*). A terminating null character is added at the end of *d*. If *n* is greater than the length of *s*, then null characters will be appended to *d* until a total of *n* characters are copied. If *n* is zero or negative, then no copy is performed.

Note that for the proper operation of *strncpy*, the length of *d* should be greater than or equal to *n*, and strings *d* and *s* should not overlap.

3.11 STRNICMP: COMPARE UP TO *n* CHARACTERS OF TWO STRINGS IGNORING CASE DIFFERENCES

```
#include <string.h>
int strnicmp(a, b)
    char *a, *b;
```

Same as *strncmp* except that case differences between the corresponding letters are ignored.

3.12 STRPBRK: FIND BREAK (DELIMITING) CHARACTER IN STRING

```
#include <string.h>
char *strpbrk(a, b)
    char *a, *b;
```

If a character from the break string *b* occurs in string *a*, then a pointer to the first occurrence of this character is returned; otherwise, the null pointer *NULL* is returned.

3.13 STRRCHR: SEARCH FOR THE LAST OCCURRENCE OF A CHARACTER

```
#include <string.h>
char *strrchr(s, c)
    char *s, c;
```

Same as *strchr* except that a pointer to the last occurrence of character *c* in string *s* is returned.

3.14 STRSPN: MEASURE SPAN (COUNT NUMBER) OF CHARACTERS IN SET

```
#include <string.h>
int strspn(a, b)
    char *a, *b;
```

Returns the number of leading characters of string *a* that are in the character set specified by string *b*.

3.15 STRTOK: GET A TOKEN

```
#include <string.h>
char *strtok(a, b)
    char *a, *b;
```

String *a* is treated as a list of tokens separated by one or more of the characters in string *b*; these characters are called the "break" or "delimiting" characters. To get tokens from a string *x* with the delimiters specified in string *y*, first call *strtok* with arguments *x* and *y*, and then call it repeatedly with the null pointer *NULL* as the first argument and *y* still as its second argument. Each time *strtok* will return a pointer to the next token from *x*. Stop calling *strtok* after it returns a *NULL* pointer which indicates that there are no more tokens in *x*, that is, the end of *x* has been reached.

4. INPUT/OUTPUT

Many C compilers provide two versions of some input routines: a function version and a macro version.

C input/output functions frequently refer to the following predefined constants which are defined in the header file *stdio.h*:

stdin	Standard input file.
stdout	Standard output file.
stderr	Standard error file.
EOF	End-of-file value (-1).
FILE ∗	Type used to declare objects that refer to files.
NULL	The null pointer.

4.1 FCLOSE: CLOSE FILE

```
#include <stdio.h>
int fclose(fp)
    FILE *fp;
```

Closes file *fp* (to be more precise, the file associated with the file pointer *fp*). If successful, *fclose* returns 0; otherwise, *EOF*. Files are automatically closed upon program termination but it is a good idea to close the files explicitly after you have finished using them. This minimizes the chances of data being lost in case of premature program termination. Also many operating systems have a limit on the number of files that can be open at any given time.

4.2 FEOF: END-OF-FILE CHECK

```
#include <stdio.h>
int feof(fp)
    FILE *fp;
```

Returns a non-zero value if the end-of-file condition is detected while reading file *fp*; otherwise, 0.

4.3 FERROR: ERROR CHECK

```
#include <stdio.h>
int ferror(fp)
    FILE *fp;
```

Returns a non-zero value if an error occurs while reading from or writing to the file *fp*; otherwise, 0.

4.4 FFLUSH: FLUSH OUTPUT BUFFER

```
#include <stdio.h>
int fflush(fp)
    FILE *fp;
```

Writes to the file *fp* any output collected in the output buffer associated with the file *fp*.

4.5 FGETC: GET A CHARACTER FROM A FILE (also see GETC)

fgetc is the function version of macro *getc*:

```
#include <stdio.h>
int fgetc(fp)
    FILE *fp;
```

Function *fgetc* returns the next character from the file *fp*, unless an end of file is encountered in which case it returns *EOF*.

4.6 FGETCHAR: GET A CHARACTER FROM STDIN (also see GETCHAR)

fgetchar is the function version of macro *getchar*.

```
#include <stdio.h>
int fgetchar()
```

Function *fgetchar* returns the next character from the standard input, unless an end of file is encountered in which case it returns *EOF*.

4.7 FGETS: GET A STRING FROM A FILE (also see GETS)

```
#include <stdio.h>
char *fgets(s, n, fp)
    char *s;
    int n;
    FILE *fp;
```

Function *fgets* reads characters from the file *fp* and stores them in the memory region pointed to by *s*. Characters are read until an end of file or a newline character is encountered, or *n* characters have been read. A terminating null character is then added at the end. Note that the newline character is stored in the string.

fgets also returns *s* as its result unless an immediate end of file is encountered or an error occurs in which case it returns the null pointer *NULL*.

4.8 FOPEN: OPEN A FILE

```
#include <stdio.h>
FILE *fopen(fname, mode)
    char *fname, mode;
```

fopen opens file *fname* (which can include path information) and returns a pointer to it. In the case *fopen* cannot open the file it returns the null pointer

NULL. Argument *mode* specifies the manner in which the file will be accessed:

"r"   Open an existing file for reading.

"w"   Create a new file or open an existing file for writing; in the latter case mark the file as empty.

"a"   Create a new file or open an existing file for writing; in the latter case the text will be appended to the file.

"r+"   Open an existing file for update (reading and writing) starting from the beginning of the file.

"w+"   Create a new file or open an existing file for updating (reading and writing); in the latter case mark the file as empty.

"a+"   Create a new file or open an existing file for updating (reading and writing); in the latter case the text will be appended to the file.

Read and write operations for files opened for updating (indicated by the character "+") must be separated by calls to *rewind* or *fseek* operations.

4.9 FPRINTF: WRITE FORMATTED OUTPUT TO A FILE (also see PRINTF & SPRINTF)

```
#include <stdio.h>
int fprintf(fp, fmt, a₁, a₂, ...)
    FILE *fp;
    char *fmt;
```

The *fprintf* function is similar to the *printf* function with one exception: *fprintf* can be used to write to any file (specified by the parameter *fp*) while *printf* writes just to standard output. See the description of *printf* for a discussion of the arguments *fmt* and a_1, a_2, and so on, and the value returned by *fprintf*.

4.10 FPUTC: WRITE A CHARACTER TO A FILE (also see PUTC & PUTCHAR)

fputc is the function version of macro *putc*:

```
#include <stdio.h>
int fputc(c, fp)
    char c;
    FILE *fp;
```

Writes character *c* to file *fp*.

4.11 FPUTS: WRITE A STRING TO A FILE (also see PUTS)

```
#include <stdio.h>
int fputs(c, fp)
    char *s;
    FILE *fp;
```

Writes string *s* (must be terminated by a null character) to file *fp*. The null character is not written. If an error occurs, function *fputs* returns −1; otherwise, 0.

4.12 FREAD: READ BLOCKS FROM A FILE

```
#include <stdio.h>
int fread(p, size, n, fp)
    char *p;
    unsigned size;
    int n;
    FILE *fp;
```

Function *fread* reads *n* blocks, each *size* bytes long, from file *fp* and stores them starting at address *p*. If an end of file is encountered before *n* complete blocks are read, then *fread* will return the number of complete blocks read; otherwise, it will return *n*.

Note that if the end of file is encountered in the middle of a block, then the partial block will be stored in the memory region pointed to by *p*. A zero value indicates that no blocks were read because an immediate end of file was encountered or because an error occurred.

4.13 FREOPEN: REOPEN A FILE

```
#include <stdio.h>
FILE *freopen(fname, mode, fp)
    char *fname, mode;
    FILE *fp;
```

Function *freopen* closes the file associated with file pointer *fp*, opens file *fname* with the access type *mode*, and associates it with *fp*. If *freopen* is successful then it returns *fp*; otherwise it returns *NULL*.

4.14 FSCANF: READ FORMATTED INPUT FROM A FILE (also see SCANF & SSCANF)

```
#include <stdio.h>
int fscanf(fp, fmt, p₁, p₂, ...)
    FILE *fp;
    char *fmt;
```

Function *fscanf* is similar to *scanf* with one exception: *fscanf* can be used to read from any file (specified by the parameter *fp*) while *scanf* reads just from standard input. See the description of *scanf* for a discussion of arguments *fmt* and p_1, p_2, and so on, and the value returned by *fscanf*.

4.15 FTELL: GET CURRENT FILE POSITION

```
#include <stdio.h>
long ftell(fp);
    FILE *fp;
```

Returns the position in file *fp* where the next read or write will occur.

4.16 FWRITE: WRITE BLOCKS TO A FILE

```
#include <stdio.h>
int fwrite(p, size, n, fp)
    char *p;
    unsigned size;
    int n;
    FILE *fp;
```

Function *fwrite* writes *n* blocks, each *size* bytes long, starting at address *p* to file *fp*. If less than *n* complete blocks are written, then *fwrite* will return the number of complete blocks written; otherwise, it will return *n*.

Note that if the file becomes full in the middle of writing a block, then a partial block will be written. A zero value indicates that no blocks were written because an immediate end of file was encountered or because an error occurred.

4.17 GETC: GET A CHARACTER FROM A FILE (also see FGETC)

getc is the macro version of function *fgetc*:

```
#include <stdio.h>
int getc(fp)
    FILE *fp;
```

Macro *getc* returns the next character from the file *fp* unless an end of file is encountered in which case it returns *EOF*.

4.18 GETCHAR: GET A CHARACTER FROM STDIN (also see FGETCHAR)

getchar is the macro version of function *fgetchar*:

```
#include <stdio.h>
int getchar()
```

Macro *getchar* returns the next character from the standard input unless an end of file is encountered in which case it returns *EOF*.

4.19 GETS: GET A STRING FROM STDIN (also see FGETS)

```
#include <stdio.h>
char *gets(s)
    char *s;
```

Function *gets* reads characters from standard input and stores them in the memory locations pointed to by *s*. Characters are read until an end-of-file or a newline character is encountered; the newline character is replaced by a terminating null character.

gets returns *s* as its result unless an immediate end of file is encountered or an error occurs, in which case it returns the null pointer *NULL*.

4.20 PRINTF: WRITE FORMATTED OUTPUT TO STDIN (also see FPRINTF & SPRINTF)

```
#include <stdio.h>
int printf(fmt, a_1, a_2, ...)
    char *fmt;
```

Function *printf* is used for writing formatted text to standard output. The output is written according to the format specified by the string *fmt* which contains the text to be printed and format items (also called conversion specifications). The format items specify the print formats and act as place holders for the expressions a_1, a_2, and so on, which are to be printed. There must be one format item for each argument a_i to be printed and vice versa.

Each format item begins with the percent character "%" and is of the form

%FlagsWidthPrecisionType

Items *Flags*, *Width*, and *Precision* are optional and may be omitted. Because of the special role of the percent character, two percent characters must be given to print a single percent character.

The optional *Flags* is a sequence of characters that modify the format specified by the other components. Zero or more flag characters can be given:

> minus (–) Left justify the item.

> plus (+) Print a leading sign (normally only a minus is printed).

> space Like plus, but a space is printed instead of a leading plus.

> sharp (#) Prefix numbers printed with octal and hexadecimal format with a 0, 0x, or 0X. For floating point formats, a decimal point is always printed.

> zero (0) Use zeros, instead of blanks, for padding.

The optional *Width* is a non-negative integer that specifies the minimum field width for the item to be printed.

The optional *Precision* is a decimal point followed by an optional integer (assumed to be zero if omitted) whose meaning depends upon the value of *Type* in the item format:

1. For integer formats (*d*, *o*, *u*, *x*, and *X*), *Precision* specifies the number of digits to be printed.

2. For the floating point format (*f*) and for the scientific formats (*e* and *E*), *Precision* specifies the number of fractional digits.

3. For the floating/scientific format (*g*), *Precision* specifies the maximum number of significant digits.

4. For the string format (*s*), *Precision* specifies the number of characters to be printed.

The *Type* component specifies the actual conversion necessary to print the corresponding argument. The conversion is specified by one of the characters listed below. Note that to print *long* arguments, the conversion character should be preceded by the letter *l*:

c   Print a character.

d   Print a decimal integer.

e   Print a double precision value (in scientific notation); note that *float* values are automatically converted to *double* before printing.

f   Print a double precision value; note that *float* values are automatically converted to *double* before printing.

E   Same as the conversion character *e* except that the exponent is preceded by an *E* instead of an *e*.

g   Print value in either *e* or *f* format as appropriate; the *e* format is used for very large or very small values.

o   Print an octal number.

s   Print a string.

u   Print an unsigned integer.

x   Print a hexadecimal integer.

Function *printf* returns the number of characters that are printed.

4.21 PUTC: WRITE A CHARACTER TO A FILE (also see FPUTC & PUTCHAR)

putc is the macro version of function *fputc*:

```
#include <stdio.h>
int putc(c, fp)
    char c;
    FILE *fp;
```

Writes character *c* to file *fp*.

4.22 PUTCHAR: WRITE A CHARACTER TO STDOUT (also see FPUTC & PUTC)

```
#include <stdio.h>
int putchar(c)
    char c;
```

Writes character c to file *stdout*.

4.23 PUTS: WRITE STRING TO STDOUT (also see FPUTS)

```
#include <stdio.h>
int fputs(s)
    char *s;
```

Writes the string s on standard output and then prints the newline character. If an error occurs, function *fputs* returns –1 ; otherwise, 0.

4.24 REWIND: RESET A FILE

```
#include <stdio.h>
int rewind(fp)
    FILE *fp;
```

Function *rewind* resets file *fp* to its beginning, that is, the file is positioned at the first byte (if any).

4.25 SCANF: READ FORMATTED INPUT FROM STDIN (also see FSCANF & SSCANF)

```
#include <stdio.h>
int scanf(fmt, p₁, p₂, ...)
    char *fmt;
```

Function *scanf* reads data from the standard input as specified by the format string *fmt* and stores it at the addresses specified by pointers p_1, p_2, and so on. The data values are read according to the items given in the string *fmt*. This string contains four classes of items:

1. White space characters which cause input to be read up to the first non-white space character in the input.

2. Format items (also called conversion specifications), which begin with the percent character %, specifying the data format and act as place holders for the pointers p_1, p_2, and so on. These pointers specify the memory locations where the data items read are to be stored.

3. Any other character which is not part of a format item must be matched by an identical character in the input.

4. To match a single percent character in the input, a pair of percent characters must be given.

There must be one format item for each argument p_i. Each format item is of the form

%*WidthType

The optional asterisk specifies a suppressed conversion. That is, the item is to be read as specified by the rest of the format item, but it is not to be stored in memory. No argument p_i is given for such an item.

Format item component *Width*, which is a non-zero unsigned decimal integer, specifies the maximum field width for the data item.

The *Type* component specifies the actual conversion necessary to read the corresponding argument. The conversion is specified by one of the characters listed below. Note that to read *long* arguments the conversion character should be preceded by the letter *l*:

   c   Read a character.

   d   Read a decimal integer.

   f   Read a double precision value (using *e*, *E*, or *g* is identical to using *f*).

   o   Read an octal number.

   s   Read a string; a white space terminates the string.

   u   Read an unsigned integer.

   x   Read a hexadecimal integer.

Function *scanf* returns the number of items read and stored in the addresses specified by the pointers p_i.

4.26 SPRINTF: WRITE FORMATTED OUTPUT TO A STRING (also see PRINTF & FPRINTF)

```
#include <stdio.h>
int sprintf(s, fmt, a₁, a₂, ...)
    char *s, *fmt;
```

Function *sprintf* is similar to *printf* with one exception: *sprintf* writes to a string (specified by the parameter *s*) while *printf* writes to the standard output. A terminating null character is added at the end of string *s*. See the description of *printf* for a discussion of arguments *fmt* and a_1, a_2, and so on, and the value returned by *sprintf*.

Function *sprintf* is used to store numeric values as text; this text can be "read" by using function *sscanf*. Functions *sprintf* and *sscanf* can thus be used to do arbitrary type conversions.

4.27 SSCANF: READ FORMATTED INPUT FROM A STRING (also see SCANF & FSCANF)

```
#include <stdio.h>
int sscanf(s, fmt, p₁, p₂, ...)
    char *s, *fmt;
```

Function *sscanf* is similar to function *scanf* with one exception: *sscanf* reads data from a string (specified by the parameter *s*) while *scanf* reads data from the standard input. See the description of *scanf* for a discussion of arguments *fmt* and p_1, p_2, and so on, and the value returned by *sscanf*. As mentioned earlier, functions *sprintf* and *sscanf* can be used to do arbitrary type conversions.

4.28 UNGETC: PUSH A CHARACTER BACK INTO THE INPUT FILE

```
#include <stdio.h>
int ungetc(c, fp)
    char c;
    FILE *fp;
```

Function *ungetc* "ungets", that is, pushes character *c* to the file *fp*. This is the character that will be first read by the next input operation. If successful, function *ungetc* returns the character pushed back; otherwise, it returns *EOF*. Note that successive calls to *getc* must be separated by at least one call to an input function, that is, there can be only one "pushed back" character at any given time.

5. INTERACTION WITH THE OPERATING SYSTEM

C compilers provide several functions for interacting with the host operating system such as the MS-DOS system.

5.1 SYSTEM: EXECUTE OPERATING SYSTEM COMMAND

```
#include <stdlib.h>
int system(cmd)
    char *cmd;
```

Executes the operating system command specified in the string *cmd*. Returns 0 if successful; otherwise, non-zero.

5.2 SIGNAL: SET UP A SIGNAL HANDLER

```
#include <signal.h>
int (*)() signal(sig, sigfun)
    int sig, (*sigfun)();
```

Function *signal* sets up the signal handler. When signal *sig* is raised, function *sigfun* will be called with *sig* as the argument. *signal* returns the old signal handler. The special predefined functions *SIG_IGN* and *SIG_DFL* respectively specify that the signal is to be ignored and that default action is to be taken.

See your C compiler reference manual for the different types of signals handled.

6. MATH LIBRARY

Some of the commonly used math library functions will be described. ANSI C may eventually have many additional math functions. For a complete list of math functions, see your C compiler reference manual.

6.1 ABS: ABSOLUTE VALUE

```
#include <math.h>
```
arithmetic-type `abs(x)`
    arithmetic-type `x;`

abs returns the absolute value of its argument. Because it is a macro, it can accept an argument of any type.

The following function versions of the *abs* macro are normally provided by many C compilers: *fabs*, *iabs*, and *labs* for computing the absolute values of *double*, *int*, and *long* arguments, respectively.

6.2 COS: COSINE

```
#include <math.h>
double cos(x)
    double x;
```

Returns the cosine of its argument x which must be in radians.

C compilers also provide functions *acos* and *cosh* to compute the arc cosine and the hyperbolic cosine.

6.3 CEIL: CEILING

```
#include <math.h>
double ceil(x)
    double x;
```

Returns the next smallest integer greater than x.

6.4 EXP: EXPONENTIATION

```
#include <math.h>
double exp(x)
    double x;
```

Returns e^x.

6.5 FLOOR: FLOOR

```
#include <math.h>
double floor(x)
    double x;
```

Returns the next largest integer smaller than *x*.

6.6 FMOD: FLOATING POINT MODULUS

```
#include <math.h>
double fmod(x, y)
    double x, y;
```

Returns the fractional part of the result of dividing *x* by *y*. Functionality is essentially similar to that of the integer operator % which is not defined for *double* values.

Function *modf* can be used to get both the integer and fractional parts of dividing *x* by *y*.

6.7 FREXP: SPLIT DOUBLE VALUE INTO FRACTION & EXPONENT

```
#include <math.h>
double frexp(v, xp)
    double v;
    int *xp;  /*pointer to exponent*/
```

Returns the fractional part (mantissa) of argument *v* and stores the exponent of *v* in *$*xp$*. The fractional part will be greater than or equal to 0.5 but less than 1.0.

Function *ldexp* does the opposite of *frexp*: it combines a fractional part and an exponent to produce a *double* value.

6.8 LOG: NATURAL LOGARITHM

```
#include <math.h>
double log(x)
    double x;
```

Returns the natural logarithm of *x*.

Function *log10* is similar to function *log* but it computes the logarithm to the base 10.

6.9 POW: RAISE TO A POWER

```
#include <math.h>
double pow(x, y)
    double x, y;
```

Returns x^y.

6.10 RAND: RANDOM NUMBER

```
#include <math.h>
int rand()
```

Returns a random number between 0 and the largest positive integer value.

The default seed value used for generating random numbers is 0. Alternative seed values can be specified by calling function *srand*.

6.11 SIN: SINE

```
#include <math.h>
double sin(x)
    double x;
```

Returns the sine of its argument which must be in radians.

C compilers also provide functions *asin* and *sinh* to compute the arc sine and the hyperbolic sine.

6.12 SQRT: SQUARE ROOT

```
#include <math.h>
double sqrt(x)
    double x;
```

Returns the square root of *x*.

6.13 TAN: TANGENT

```
#include <math.h>
double tan(x)
    double x;
```

Returns the tangent of its argument which must be in radians.

C compilers also provide functions *atan* and *tanh* to compute the arc tangent and the hyperbolic tangent.

APPENDIX 2

ASCII CHARACTER SET

Character	Decimal Value	Octal Value	Hexadecimal Value
^@ *(nul)*	0	0	0
^A *(soh)*	1	1	1
^B *(stx)*	2	2	2
^C *(etx)*	3	3	3
^D *(eot)*	4	4	4
^E *(enq)*	5	5	5
^F *(ack)*	6	6	6
^G *(bel)*	7	7	7
^H *(bs)*	8	10	8
^I *(tab)*	9	11	9
^J *(lf)*	10	12	A
^K *(vt)*	11	13	B
^L *(ff)*	12	14	C
^M *(cr)*	13	15	D
^N *(so)*	14	16	E
^O *(si)*	15	17	F
^P *(dle)*	16	20	10
^Q *(dc1)*	17	21	11
^R *(dc2)*	18	22	12
^S *(dc3)*	19	23	13
^T *(dc4)*	20	24	14
^U *(nak)*	21	25	15
^V *(syn)*	22	26	16

Character	Decimal Value	Octal Value	Hexadecimal Value
^W *(etb)*	23	27	17
^X *(can)*	24	30	18
^Y *(em)*	25	31	19
^Z *(sub)*	26	32	1A
^[*(esc)*	27	33	1B
^\ *(fs)*	28	34	1C
^] *(gs)*	29	35	1D
^^ *(rs)*	30	36	1E
^_ *(us)*	31	37	1F
space	32	40	20
!	33	41	21
"	34	42	22
#	35	43	23
$	36	44	24
%	37	45	25
&	38	46	26
'	39	47	27
(	40	50	28
)	41	51	29
*	42	52	2A
+	43	53	2B
,	44	54	2C
-	45	55	2D
.	46	56	2E
/	47	57	2F
0	48	60	30
1	49	61	31
2	50	62	32
3	51	63	33
4	52	64	34
5	53	65	35
6	54	66	36

Character	Decimal Value	Octal Value	Hexadecimal Value
7	55	67	37
8	56	70	38
9	57	71	39
:	58	72	3A
;	59	73	3B
<	60	74	3C
=	61	75	3D
>	62	76	3E
?	63	77	3F
@	64	100	40
A	65	101	41
B	66	102	42
C	67	103	43
D	68	104	44
E	69	105	45
F	70	106	46
G	71	107	47
H	72	110	48
I	73	111	49
J	74	112	4A
K	75	113	4B
L	76	114	4C
M	77	115	4D
N	78	116	4E
O	79	117	4F
P	80	120	50
Q	81	121	51
R	82	122	52
S	83	123	53
T	84	124	54
U	85	125	55
V	86	126	56

Character	Decimal Value	Octal Value	Hexadecimal Value
W	87	127	57
X	88	130	58
Y	89	131	59
Z	90	132	5A
[	91	133	5B
\	92	134	5C
]	93	135	5D
^	94	136	5E
_	95	137	5F
`	96	140	60
a	97	141	61
b	98	142	62
c	99	143	63
d	100	144	64
e	101	145	65
f	102	146	66
g	103	147	67
h	104	150	68
i	105	151	69
j	106	152	6A
k	107	153	6B
l	108	154	6C
m	109	155	6D
n	110	156	6E
o	111	157	6F
p	112	160	70
q	113	161	71
r	114	162	72
s	115	163	73
t	116	164	74
u	117	165	75
v	118	166	76

Character	Decimal Value	Octal Value	Hexadecimal Value
w	119	167	77
x	120	170	78
y	121	171	79
z	122	172	7A
{	123	173	7B
|	124	174	7C
}	125	175	7D
~	126	176	7E
del	127	177	7F

BIBLIOGRAPHY

ANSI83]   *American National Standard Pascal Computer Programming Language. IEEE*, 1983.

[Byte83]   C is the theme of the August 1983 issue of *Byte Magazine*.

[Coop83]   Cooper, D. *Standard Pascal User Reference Manual*. W. W. Norton & Co., 1983.

[Feue84]   Feuer, A. and N. Gehani (Editors). *Comparing and Assessing Programming Languages: Ada, C & Pascal*. Prentice-Hall, 1984.

[Geha85]   Gehani, N. *C for Personal Computers*. Computer Science Press, 1985.

[Harb84]   Harbison, S. P. and G. L. Steele, Jr. *A C Reference Manual*. Prentice-Hall, 1984.

[IBM83a]   *IBM DOS* (by Microsoft). IBM Personal Computer Language Series. Item no. 1502343, 1983.

[IBM83b]   *IBM DOS Technical Reference Manual* (by Microsoft). IBM Personal Computer Language Series. Item no. 6024125, 1983.

[Jens78]   Jensen, K. and N. Wirth. *Pascal User Manual and Report*. Springer-Verlag 1978.

[Kern78]   Kernighan, B. W. and D. M. Ritchie. *The C Programming Language*. Prentice-Hall, 1978.

[Knut78]   Knuth, D. E. *The Art of Computer Programming (Volume 2)*. Addison-Wesley, 1969.

[Latt86]   *Lattice C Compiler for MS-DOS. Programmer's Reference Manual*, Volumes 1 and 2, 1986.

[Phra83]   Phraner, R. A. Nine C compilers for the IBM PC. *Byte*, Volume 8, Number 8, August 1983.

[Plum83]   Plum, T. *Learning to Program in C*. Plum Hall, 1983.

[TPas85]   *Turbo Pascal (version 3.0) Reference Manual*. Borland International, 1985.

INDEX

W